To Don
Cook Well
Eat Well
Be Well

FARMHOUSE KITCHEN
FAVORITES

Favorite Recipes *and* Fondest Memories
from The Farmhouse Kitchen

www.farmhousekitchen.us

PUBLISHED BY FOUR CROWS, INC., FOR FARMHOUSE KITCHEN

For bulk purchase of this book, go to www.farmhousekitchen.us

Paula S. Croteau is available for group speaking engagements, consultations, and book signings. www.farmhousekitchen.us

Designed by Michael Croteau, Cro2, Inc. www.Cro2.com
Photography by Michael Croteau
Printed by Quad Graphics in the United States of America
Many of the fabrics in this book provided by Duralee Fabrics, Ltd. www.Duralee.com

Publisher's Cataloging-in-Publication data

Croteau, Paula S.
Farmhouse kitchen favorites: my favorite recipes and fondest memories from the farmhouse kitchen / Paula S. Croteau; foreword by Lettie Teague.
p. cm.
ISBN 978-0-9830753-0-1
1. Cookery, American. 2. Cooking, American. 3. Farm life - United States - History - 20th century - Anecdotes. I. Teague, Lettie. II. Title.

TX715 .C942 2010
641.5-dc22   2010939364

WHEN I WALK INTO MY KITCHEN, I NEVER FEEL ALONE. I BRING WITH ME A LIFETIME OF LOVE AND MEMORIES OF EVERY MEAL SHARED. FOOD TO ME IS NEVER JUST FOOD. IT TOUCHES ALL OF MY SENSES AND NEVER LETS ME DOWN. THE PROCESS AND RESULTS TELL ME: WHO I AM, WHO I HAVE BEEN AND WHO I WANT TO BE. NEVER THE SAME JOURNEY, NEVER THE SAME RESULTS, YET ALWAYS SATISFYING. COOKING FEEDS MY PASSION AND NOURISHES MY SOUL.

~Paula S. Croteau, "The Farmer's Daughter"~

Dedication

CHESTER H. SKWARA

THIS COOKBOOK COULD ONLY BE DEDICATED TO ONE PERSON:
"GRAMPS." MY KITCHEN COMPANION EVERY STEP OF THE WAY
AND THE PERSON THAT EVERY COOK WANTS BY THEIR SIDE.
A MASTER OF THE CHEF'S KNIFE WHOSE PASSIONS ARE EQUALLY
FRUITS AND VEGETABLES. THERE IS NOTHING MORE BEAUTIFUL
TO HIM THAN THE BOUNTY OF A GARDEN AND NO PLACE MORE
BEAUTIFUL THAN THE NORTH FORK. I HAVE TO AGREE—WITH
ONE EXCEPTION. THERE IS ONE THING MORE BEAUTIFUL TO
ME, THE SIGHT OF MY FATHER IN THE KITCHEN, HIS
UNIVERSE. THANK YOU DAD, I'M SO GLAD THAT I AM YOUR
FARMER'S DAUGHTER.

"CULINARY ROLE MODEL AND PAL"

hen I moved to the North Fork of Long Island in the autumn of 2009, I thought I was lucky to have found a house less than half a mile from the beach and close to the vineyards. The latter, after all, was what had first inspired my relocation from New York. As a longtime wine journalist I'd gotten to know some of the local winemakers over the years. But there were also vintners I didn't know, including Paula and Michael Croteau of Croteaux Vineyards and The Farmhouse Kitchen Cooking School.

"You have to meet Paula Croteau," Louisa Hargrave said to me soon after my move. (Louisa is the matriarch of Long Island winemaking; she was first to plant grapes on the North Fork.) "Paula is practically your neighbor. You'll like her; she's great," Louisa added. It turned out that Louisa was as prescient about people as she was about grapes. I liked Paula and I thought she was great.

Paula was great when I asked her a few simple questions about knife skills. (I'm not much of a cook.) She was great when it came to eating dinner at my house—and actually seeming to enjoy it. (See note in previous parentheses.) She was great when it came to feeding me—and my friends. In fact, she fed just about anyone I brought to her door. This meant that Paula's cooking was all my friends talked about for the rest of their visit. "Paula's lobster tails were amazing," they'd say afterwards. "What a spectacular risotto Paula made," they'd marvel weeks later. Paula's cooking became not only my great inspiration but also my secret trump card.

Paula was also great when it came to encouraging words—as much in life as with food. "Cooking is about sharing. It's not about the food. It's about love," Paula said to me in the same soothing tone she employs when talking to her students. (I know because I've been to her classroom too.) And I know from Paula that's not just a line but a bedrock belief that her cooking school, her family, her life, is founded upon. And she is a (very big) reason why I feel so fortunate to call the North Fork my home.

Lettie Teague
Wine Columnist, *The Wall Street Journal*

TABLE OF CONTENTS

DEDICATION   5

FOREWORD   7

FARMHOUSE MEMORIES

When I Walk Into My Kitchen   3

Grease and Stains   10

My Wooden Spoons   34

See You With Your Apron On   52

Competing With Yoga   70

Food Is Love   90

The More Butter the Better   112

Coming Full Circle   132

FARMHOUSE FAVORITES & FACTS

In My Pantry   150

Abbreviations   151

Kitchen Tools   151

Recipe Terms   152

Dos & Don'ts   153

Stores, Markets,
Gardens & Websites   154

THANK YOU   156

INDEX   158

RECIPES

FARMHOUSE RECIPES

APPETIZERS "My Weakness"   11

SOUPS & SALADS "It's That Simple"   35

RICE, GRAINS & BEANS "Never Look Back"   53

CASSEROLES & ONE POTS "Comfort Food Nirvana"   71

MEATS & SEAFOOD "An Edible Sponge"   91

DESSERTS "Lasting Impression"   113

BREAKFAST & BREADS "You Can't Miss"   133

"GREASE & STAINS"

I HOPE THAT THIS COOKBOOK WILL SOON BE COVERED WITH GREASE AND STAINS. THEN IT WILL TRULY HAVE BEEN OF SERVICE, YOUR TRUSTED COMPANION AND "LIFELINE" WHEN COMPANY CALLS. I HAVE A LIBRARY OF COOKBOOKS, BUT THERE ARE ONLY A FEW THAT I CAN TRUST. THAT IS MY WISH FOR YOU AND THIS COOKBOOK. THAT IT BECOMES YOUR FAVORITE, SPLATTERED WITH FOOD AND DOG-EARED FROM USE.

Appetizers

"MY WEAKNESS"

ANYONE WHO KNOWS ME WELL KNOWS THAT APPETIZERS ARE MY WEAKNESS. THEY ARE TINY, DELECTABLE MOUTHFULS THAT EXPLODE WITH FLAVOR. SIMPLISTIC IN HOW THEY'RE PRESENTED, YET DEEPLY SATISFYING. OFTEN FILLING ENOUGH TO SKIP THE MEAL, WHICH IS WHY LESS IS TRULY MORE. ONE OR TWO CHOICES ARE MORE THAN ENOUGH. I LOVE THE SIMPLICITY OF SERVING JUST OLIVES AND NUTS. IN FACT, THAT'S WHAT I'LL BE SERVING WHEN YOU COME TO MY HOUSE.

Farmhouse Cheese Spread 13, Green Grape Salsa 15, Feta with Roasted Grapes 17,
Zucchini Quiche 19, Eggplant Caponata 21, Barbecued Chorizo 23,
Cheddar Cheese Crackers 25, Red Onion Galette 27, Olives with a Twist 29,
Roasted Nuts & Fruit 31, Croteaux Rosé Sangria 33

Farmhouse Cheese Spread

FARMHOUSE CHEESE SPREAD

1- 8oz Container Cream Cheese
1/4 Cup Roquefort or Blue Cheese, crumbled
1/4 Cup Red Onion or Scallion, finely chopped
1/4 Cup dried Currants
1 tsp Herbes de Provence
1 Tb small Capers
1 Tb Sun-Dried Tomatoes, finely chopped
1/4 Cup Pine Nuts, toasted
Sprig of fresh Rosemary, to garnish

- In a bowl, mix together all ingredients, except nuts,
  until combined.
- Transfer into a ramekin or form a ball with
  dampened hands.
- Cover with plastic wrap and refrigerate until solid.
- Top ramekin or roll cheese ball in pine nuts when ready to serve.
- Garnish with a sprig of rosemary.
- Bring to room temperature, serve with baguette and fruit.

Makes 1 1/2 Cups

FROM THE KITCHEN OF: RACHEL CURRERI
*Attending Paula's classes
is like a spa day for me.*

Green Grape Salsa

GREEN GRAPE SALSA

2 Cups Green Grapes, cut into small pieces
1/4 Cup Red Onion or Scallion, finely chopped
1 Jalapeno Pepper, seeded and finely chopped, to taste
2 Tb fresh Mint or Cilantro
2 tsp fresh Lime Juice
1/4 tsp coarse Salt
1-2 Tb Honey

- In a bowl, mix together grapes, onion, jalapeno and fresh herbs.
- Add lime juice, salt and honey.
- Gently mix until combined.
- Can be made up to 4 hours ahead of time, covered and refrigerated.
- Bring to room temperature before serving.
- Serve in tortilla cups or with tortilla chips.

* Delicious served with grilled chicken, fish or pork!

Makes 2 cups

Feta with Roasted Grapes

FETA WITH ROASTED GRAPES

1 Lb Feta Cheese, cut into 1/2-inch cubes
1 large bunch Red Grapes, stems removed
1-2 Tb Extra Virgin Olive Oil
Salt & Pepper, to taste
2-3 Tb Honey
Fresh cracked Black Pepper, to taste
1/2 Cup Pine Nuts, toasted

- Preheat oven to 425 degrees.
- Place separated grapes on a Silpat-lined, rimmed cookie sheet.
- Drizzle grapes with olive oil, sprinkle with salt & pepper.
- Roast the grapes in the oven until wilted, approximately
  10–15 minutes.
- Shake the pan and roll the grapes every 5 minutes.
- Toast pine nuts in a small skillet over medium-high heat.
- Stir continually until golden, about 3–5 minutes.
- Place cheese cubes on a decorative platter.
- Top each cube with a roasted grape.
- Drizzle with honey and top with fresh cracked black pepper.
- Spear the cheese and grapes with a decorative toothpick.
- Sprinkle nuts on top of each cube.
- Serve at room temperature.

* Grapes and cheese can be assembled and refrigerated ahead of time.
  Drizzle with honey, pepper and nuts just before serving.

Makes 18-24 servings

FROM THE KITCHEN OF: CATHY KIDD

Paula taught me how to bring ingredients, skill, laughter, excitement and camaraderie together, so that now cooking is a celebration of togetherness. I am forever grateful.

Zucchini Quiche

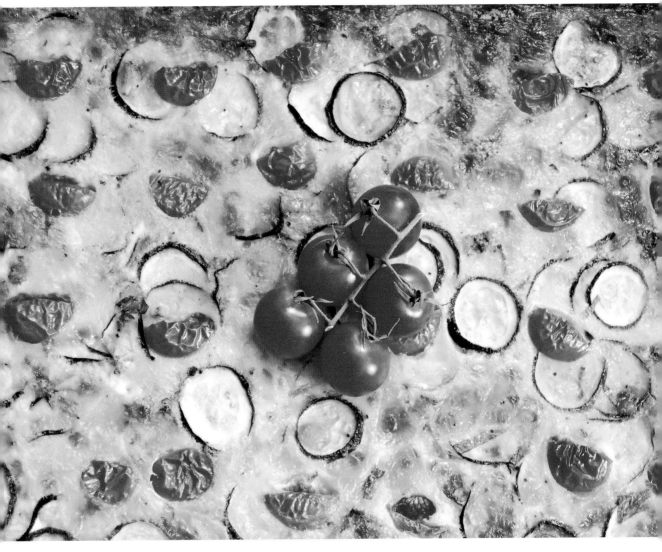

Zucchini Quiche

2 packages store-bought Crescent Rolls
2 tsp Honey Dijon Mustard
4 Tb unsalted Butter, cut into 1/2-inch pieces
1 medium Yellow Onion, chopped
1 clove Garlic, chopped
3 medium Zucchini, thinly sliced
2 Tb fresh Parsley, chopped
1 Tb fresh Basil, chopped
1 tsp fresh Oregano, chopped or 1/2 tsp dried Oregano
1/2 tsp Salt
1/4 tsp Pepper
6 large Eggs, lightly beaten
1 Cup Mozzarella Cheese or cheese of your choice, grated
1 Cup Cherry Tomatoes, cut in quarters

- Preheat oven to 375 degrees.
- Spread crescent rolls onto a rimmed sheet pan.
- Using kitchen scissors cut and arrange the dough to cover the bottom and sides of the pan.
- Spread mustard on the dough and set aside.
- In a skillet, melt the butter.
- Add onions and garlic, sauté until soft.
- Add zucchini and sauté until just softened, about 5 minutes.
- Remove from heat and stir in all the herbs, salt and pepper.
- Let the zucchini mixture cool.
- In a medium bowl, mix together the eggs and cheese.
- Stir in the cooled zucchini mixture and pour evenly over the crescent rolls.
- Space the cherry tomatoes on top of the quiche to create a grid for cutting.
- Bake for 30 minutes or until the quiche is golden.
- Cover with foil for the last 10 minutes if the quiche starts to get too brown.
- Cool on a wire rack.
- Once cooled, cut into squares and place the quiche on a decorative platter.

* Can be made in a pie plate and served as a classic quiche.

Makes 24 servings

Eggplant Caponata

EGGPLANT CAPONATA

2 Cups cubed Eggplant and/or Zucchini
1 tsp Salt
4 Tb Extra Virgin Olive Oil
1 large Yellow Onion, chopped
1/2 Cup Red Pepper, chopped
2 Celery stalks, chopped
1- 28oz can Plum Tomatoes, crushed or 2 cups fresh
  Plum Tomatoes, chopped
1/4 tsp Pepper
1 tsp dried Oregano
1/2 tsp dried Basil or 6 leaves fresh Basil, finely sliced
  (leaves added when caponata cools)
2 cloves Garlic, minced
1 Tb fresh Italian Parsley, chopped
1/2 Cup pitted Kalamata Olives, chopped
2 Tb Capers, drained
1/2 Cup Pine Nuts, toasted
1/2 Cup White Raisins

- In a colander, sprinkle and toss eggplant and/or zucchini with salt and let drain in the sink for 30 minutes.
- In a heavy cast iron pot, heat oil on medium-high heat.
- Add onions, peppers, celery and eggplant all at once and sauté for 10 minutes, until vegetables are soft.
- Add tomatoes and remaining ingredients and bring to a boil.
- Lower heat to medium-low and simmer the caponata until vegetables are tender, about 45 minutes, stirring every 10–15 minutes.
- If mixture starts sticking to the bottom of the pot, add more tomatoes or tomato juice.
- Serve warm or at room temperature with grilled bread.

Makes 6 cups

Barbecued Chorizo

2 Tb Extra Virgin Olive Oil
1 1/2 Lb Chorizo or Kielbasa, cut into 1/4-inch slices
2/3 Cup dry Red Wine
1/2 tsp fresh Thyme leaves or 1/4 tsp dried Thyme
1/4 Cup Chili Sauce
1 Tb Light Brown Sugar
1 Tb Cider Vinegar

- Heat oil in a large non-stick skillet until very hot.
- Add meat and fry for 1 minute on each side.
- Remove the meat from the pan and place in a bowl.
- Add remaining ingredients to the skillet and simmer and stir until
  sauce is reduced and thickened, approximately 10 minutes.
- Pour the sauce over the meat and garnish with fresh thyme.
- Serve hot or at room temperature.

*Add 1/2 tsp Smoked Paprika if using Kielbasa.

Makes 4-6 servings

Cheddar Cheese Crackers

CHEDDAR CHEESE CRACKERS

1 Cup Pecans, toasted
1 Cup plus 1 Tb unsalted Butter, softened and cut
   into 1/2-inch pieces
1 Lb Cheddar Cheese or cheese of your choice, grated
2 Cups Unbleached White Flour
1 Cup Dried Cranberries
1/4 tsp Cayenne Pepper, to taste
Pinch of Salt

- Toast pecans on a rimmed cookie sheet for 10–12 minutes, until aromatic and golden.
- In a bowl, mix the warm toasted pecans with 1 tablespoon of butter then chop.
- In a food processor, using the blade attachment, mix the 1 cup of butter and grated cheese
  until crumbly.
- Add nuts, flour, cranberries, cayenne and salt.
- Mix until a ball forms.
- Divide dough into 4 pieces.
- Place dough on a sheet of wax paper.
- Roll into 4, 12-inch by 1-inch logs.
- Freeze for 30 minutes or chill overnight.
- Preheat oven to 350 degrees.
- Cut logs with a sharp knife into 1/4-inch thick slices and place on a Silpat-lined
  cookie sheet, 2 inches apart.
- Bake for 10–12 minutes, or until golden.

Makes 8 dozen crackers

RED ONION GALETTE

3 large Red Onions, peeled and thinly sliced
2 Tb unsalted Butter
1/4 Cup Olive Oil
1/2 tsp dried Thyme
1 Tb Sugar
Salt & Pepper, to taste
1 Cup dry Red Wine
Sprig of fresh Thyme
1 Recipe Flaky Pie Crust (page 121) or
1 store-bought Pie Crust

- In a large bowl, soak the sliced onions in a cold water bath for 20 minutes.
- Drain onions in a colander and set aside.
- In a large skillet, heat butter and oil on medium-high heat until combined.
- Add onions, thyme and sugar to the oil.
- Sauté until the onions are wilted and tender, about 10–15 minutes.
- Add wine to the onion mixture and continue cooking over medium-high heat
  until liquid evaporates.
- Season well with salt & pepper.
- Cool the onion mixture completely.
- Preheat the oven to 425 degrees.
- Roll pie crust into a large circle and place on a Silpat-lined unrimmed baking sheet.
- Crimp the edges of the crust.
- Spread onion mixture evenly on top of the crust.
- Bake galette for 30 minutes, or until the crust and onions are golden.
- Using a large angled spatula, slide the galette onto a wire rack to cool.

Makes 8 servings

*For small bite size galettes, cut the dough with a round 2-inch biscuit cutter and
  evenly space on a Silpat-lined baking sheet.
- Using a small ice cream scoop, top the dough with the finely chopped onion mixture.
- Bake for 15–20 minutes or until the crust and onions are golden.
- Top with a sprig of fresh thyme.

Makes 24-36 mini galettes

OLIVES WITH A TWIST

2 Cups assorted Olives
1 tsp Orange zest
1 tsp Lemon zest
1 clove Garlic, minced
2 Tb fresh Parsley, chopped
1 Tb fresh Rosemary, chopped
1 tsp fresh Oregano, chopped
1/2 tsp fresh Ginger, grated
1/4 tsp Fennel seeds
1/2 tsp Salt
1/4 tsp Pepper
2 Tb Extra Virgin Olive Oil

- In a decorative bowl, combine all ingredients except olive oil with the olives.
- Drizzle with olive oil and mix well.
- Serve at room temperate with a small bowl for pits.

* Can be stored in the refrigerator up to one month.
- Cover olives with olive oil.
- Use a slotted spoon to transfer olives to a bowl.

Makes 2 cups

FROM THE KITCHEN OF: MONIQUE STANTON

*Paula's gracious presence is
matched by her love of food
and her love of people.*

Roasted Nuts & Fruit

1 1/4 Lb Almonds, Pecans or Walnuts, toasted
1 Tb fresh Rosemary, finely chopped
1/4 tsp Cayenne Pepper, or to taste
2 tsp Light Brown Sugar
1 tsp coarse Salt
1 Tb unsalted Butter, melted
1 Cup dried Cherries, Cranberries or Blueberries

- Preheat oven to 350 degrees.
- Toast nuts on a rimmed baking sheet for 10–15 minutes, or until aromatic and golden.
- In a bowl, toss together the rosemary, cayenne pepper, brown sugar, salt and butter.
- Toss warm nuts with the rosemary mixture and stir in dried fruit.
- Spread nut and berry mixture on a Silpat or parchment-lined baking sheet.
- When cool, break nut and berry mixture apart.
- Serve in a decorative bowl.

Makes 4 cups

Croteaux Rosé Sangria

CROTEAUX ROSÉ SANGRIA

1 Bottle Croteaux Rosé
2 Cups Guava Juice or other tropical juice
1/2 Cup plus 2 Tb Grand Marnier or Orange Liquor
3/4 Cup Sugar
3/4 tsp Cinnamon
1/4 tsp Salt
Fresh Fruit slices (Apples, Oranges)
Cinnamon stick, for garnish

- In a pitcher combine Rosé, fruit juice, liquor, 1/2 cup sugar and 1/2 tsp cinnamon.
- Let mixture macerate in the refrigerator for 2 hours or overnight.
- Combine the remaining 1/4 cup sugar, 1/4 tsp cinnamon and salt in a saucer.
- Place the remaining 2 Tb liquor in another saucer.
- Dip glasses in the liquor, then into the sugar mixture.
  (Glasses can be rimmed the night before to allow sugar to harden).
- Fill rimmed glasses with lots of ice and then pour in sangria.
- Garnish with fresh fruit and a cinnamon stick.

*Freeze whole fruit and use to chill Sangria in a bowl or pitcher!

Makes 6-8 glasses

"MY WOODEN SPOONS"

I'M ESPECIALLY FOND OF WOODEN SPOONS. MINE HAVE STIRRED HUNDREDS OF SOUPS AND STEWS. THEY ARE WELL WORN FROM USE, BUT HAPPY AND CONTENT IN THEIR PLACE OF HONOR BY THE STOVE. ALWAYS THERE WHEN YOU NEED THEM, ALWAYS READY FOR THE JOB AT HAND. I ESPECIALLY CHERISH MY GRANDMOTHERS' SPOONS. MISSHAPEN AND CRACKED, BUT STILL STURDY, THEY PROUDLY SHOW THEIR CULINARY PAST. I USE THEM ONLY ON VERY SPECIAL OCCASIONS, KNOWING MY GRANDMOTHERS WATCH OVER MY COOKING THROUGH THEIR PASSED-DOWN WOODEN SPOONS.

Soups & Salads

"IT'S THAT SIMPLE"

THE NUMBER ONE PHONE CALL I RECEIVE FROM MY STUDENTS IS, "WHAT DO I SERVE MY GUESTS?" THE MOTHER-IN-LAW WHO HAS NEVER LIKED YOU, LET ALONE YOUR COOKING; FRIENDS FROM COLLEGE WHO HAVE BEEN TO CULINARY SCHOOL; OR YOUR BOOK CLUB MEMBERS WHO ALWAYS SEEM TO OUTDO THEMSELVES. I CAN FEEL THE TENSION OVER THE PHONE LINE AND SEE THE COOKBOOKS SPREAD OUT ON THE KITCHEN TABLE. AFTER LISTENING INTENTLY, FOOD THERAPIST THAT I AM, "SOUP & SALAD" I SAY! THERE'S ONLY DEAD AIR ON THE OTHER END OF THE PHONE LINE. MY STUDENT IS SO TAKEN ABACK THAT THE ANSWER COULD BE AS SIMPLE AS SOUP & SALAD. "IMPOSSIBLE," I CAN HEAR THEIR "I MUST BE MARTHA" MINDS REGISTERING. I GENTLY SAY IT AGAIN, "SOUP & SALAD." NOTHING CALMS THE NERVES AND FILLS THE SOUL BETTER THAN A BOWL OF HOMEMADE SOUP AND A SATISFYING SALAD. THE VELVETY BROTH AND LAYERING OF FLAVORS INSTANTLY APPEALS TO ALL GUESTS. AND BEFORE YOU KNOW IT YOU'RE CHATTING ABOUT ALL THE PEOPLE AND MEMORIES THAT BROUGHT YOU TOGETHER IN THE FIRST PLACE. IT'S AS SIMPLE AS SOUP & SALAD.

North Fork Potato & Leek Soup 37, Seafood Corn Chowder 39, Zucchini Basil Soup 41,
Carrot Ginger Soup 43, Farmhouse Green Salad and Vinaigrette 45,
Grapefruit, Fennel & Arugula Salad 47, Iceberg Wedge with Creamy Blue Cheese 49,
Roasted Asparagus Salad 51

6 Tb unsalted Butter

4 Leeks, white ends only, cleaned and chopped

2 Yellow Apples, peeled and cubed

4 Yukon Gold Potatoes, peeled and cubed

4 Cups organic Chicken Stock

2 Cups Kielbasa, halved and cut into 1/2-inch pieces

2 Cups Half & Half

Salt & Pepper, to taste

Fresh grated Nutmeg, to taste

1 Baguette, cut into 1-inch pieces and toasted

1- 8oz package Cream Cheese, cut into 6 cubes

2 Tb fresh Flat Leaf Parsley, chopped

- In a large heavy pot, melt butter on medium-high heat.

- Add leeks and apples, sauté until soft.

- Add potatoes and stock.

- Cover soup and bring to a boil.

- Reduce heat to medium.

- Cook until potatoes are tender, 15-20 minutes.

- Add kielbasa and stir in half & half.

- Season with salt, pepper and nutmeg, then gently reheat.

- Top toasted baguette with cream cheese cubes and place on the bottom of the soup bowls.

- Ladle hot soup on top.

- Garnish with fresh parsley.

Makes 6 cups

FROM THE KITCHEN OF: CAROL BARTHOLOMEW

My experience with Paula has been like having a gifted, warm relative share their best kept secrets.

Seafood Corn Chowder

SEAFOOD CORN CHOWDER

1/2 Lb Bacon, cut into 1/2-inch pieces
1 large Yellow Onion, chopped
2 stalks Celery, chopped
1 Red Pepper, chopped
2 Tb Unbleached White Flour
4 Cups organic Chicken or Seafood Stock
2 Potatoes, peeled and diced
2 Cups fresh or frozen Corn kernels
1/2 tsp dried Thyme
2 Cups Half & Half
Salt & Pepper, to taste
1/2 Lb Bay Scallops
1-2 Tb unsalted Butter
Fresh Flat Leaf Parsley, for garnish
6 Kaiser Rolls

- In a large heavy pot on medium-high heat, cook bacon until it begins to brown.
- Remove all but 2 Tb of bacon fat.
- Add onion, celery and peppers to the bacon and sauté until soft.
- Add flour, cook and stir for 2 minutes.
- Add stock, potatoes, corn and thyme.
- Bring soup to a boil.
- Cover and reduce heat to medium.
- Cook until potatoes are just tender, 15-20 minutes.
- Meanwhile, wash and pat dry scallops and season with salt & pepper.
- Melt butter in a skillet and sear scallops for 2-3 minutes each side, until golden-crusted.
- Remove soup from the stove.
- Add the seared scallops, half & half and salt & pepper, to taste.
- Ladle soup into the toasted Kaiser rolls.
- Sprinkle with fresh parsley.

Makes 6 cups

TOASTED KAISER ROLLS:
- Preheat oven to 350 degrees.
- Cut thin top of the Kaiser rolls off and reserve.
- Scoop out the soft center of the roll using a spoon.
- Brush the inside of the roll and the "tops" with olive oil and sprinkle with salt & pepper.
- Place rolls on a rimmed baking sheet.
- Toast rolls and "tops" in the oven for 10-15 minutes, or until crisp and golden.

Zucchini Basil Soup

ZUCCHINI BASIL SOUP

4 Tb unsalted Butter
  or 2 Tb unsalted Butter and 2 Tb Extra Virgin Olive Oil
1 large Yellow Onion, chopped
2 cloves Garlic, chopped
4 Cups organic Chicken or Vegetable Stock
3 medium Zucchini, cut into 1/2-inch pieces (6 cups)
1- 8 oz package Cream Cheese, cut into cubes
1 tsp Lemon zest
2 Tb fresh Basil, chopped
Salt & Pepper, to taste

- In a large heavy pot, melt butter on medium-high heat.
- Add onion and garlic, sauté until soft.
- Add stock and zucchini.
- Bring the soup to a boil.
- Shut off heat and cover.
- Let soup rest on the stove for 15 minutes.
- Add cream cheese, lemon zest, salt, pepper and basil.
- Puree soup with a hand blender until smooth and creamy.
- Serve soup hot or chilled.
- Garnish with fresh basil leaves and lemon wheels.

Makes 6 cups

FROM THE KITCHEN OF: WENDY CARLEY

*My first impression upon entering
Paula's kitchen was how warm and
welcoming the atmosphere was.
I knew that this would be an
extraordinary experience and
I was not disappointed.*

Carrot Ginger Soup

CARROT GINGER SOUP

6 Tb unsalted Butter
  or 3 Tb unsalted Butter and 3 Tb Extra Virgin Olive Oil
1 large Yellow Onion, chopped
3 cloves Garlic, minced
1-inch fresh Ginger, smashed
1/2 tsp Curry Powder
4 Cups organic Chicken or Vegetable Stock
1 Lb Carrots, peeled & cut to 1/2-inch pieces
2 Tb fresh Lemon Juice
Salt & Pepper, to taste
Candied Ginger, for garnish
Fresh Cilantro or Parsley, chopped

- In a large heavy pot, melt butter on medium heat.
- Add onion, garlic, and ginger and sauté until soft.
- Add curry, cook and stir for 1 minute.
- Add stock and carrots.
- Bring soup to a boil.
- Cover soup and reduce heat to medium.
- Cook until carrots are tender, 15–20 minutes.
- Remove smashed ginger.
- Puree soup with a hand blender until soup is smooth and creamy.
- Stir in lemon juice, salt & pepper.
- Serve soup hot or chilled.
- Garnish with cilantro or parsley and slivered candied ginger.

Makes 6 cups

Farmhouse Green Salad

6 Cups organic Greens (Baby Greens, Romaine, Mache or Butter Lettuce)
1 Cup Fresh Fruit, sliced (Peaches, Berries or Apples)
1/2 Cup Nuts, toasted (Pine Nuts, Pecans or Walnuts)
1/2 Cup Cheese, crumbled (Chevre, Roquefort or Parmesan)

- Place washed greens in a decorative bowl.
- Top with fruit, nuts and cheese.
- Place the vinaigrette in a pitcher.
- Lightly dress and toss the salad just before serving.

Makes 4-6 servings

Classic French Vinaigrette

3/4 Cup Canola Oil
1/4 Cup White Wine Vinegar
1 tsp Dijon Mustard
1 tsp of Sugar or to taste
Salt & Pepper, to taste

- Place oil in a pitcher.
- Rapidly whisk in vinegar, mustard, sugar, salt and pepper until creamy.
- Store in covered jar in the refrigerator for later use.

Makes 1 cup

Farmhouse Vinaigrette

3/4 Cup Canola Oil
1 Tb roasted Nut Oil
1/4 Cup Rice Wine Vinegar
1/2 tsp Dijon Mustard
1-2 Tb Fruit Jam
Salt & Pepper, to taste

- Place oil in a pitcher.
- Rapidly whisk in vinegar, mustard, jam, salt & pepper until creamy.

*If using blueberries in the salad, use blueberry jam; peaches, peach jam; oranges, marmalade.

Makes 1 cup

GRAPEFRUIT, FENNEL & ARUGULA SALAD

1/4 Lb organic baby Arugula leaves
1 medium bulb Fennel, cored and thinly sliced
2 Pink Grapefruits or Oranges, peeled and sectioned
1 small Red Onion, cut into thin slivers
1/4 Cup Pine Nuts, toasted
1/4 Cup Parmigiana Reggiano shavings
1/2 Cup Extra Virgin Olive Oil
1/4 Cup fresh Grapefruit or Orange Juice
1 Tb Honey Dijon Mustard
Salt & Pepper, to taste

- In a large colorful bowl, layer the arugula, fennel and citrus.
- Top with nuts and cheese shavings.
- In a pitcher, rapidly whisk together the oil, citrus juice, Dijon, salt & pepper until creamy.
- Just before serving, drizzle citrus vinaigrette over the salad and gently toss.

Makes 4-6 servings

VARIATION:

- Replace Citrus with assorted thin Melon slices.
- Replace Parmigiana Reggiano with Goat Cheese.
- Replace Citrus juice with Mango juice.
- All other ingredients remain the same.

Iceberg Wedge with Creamy Blue Cheese

ICEBERG WEDGE WITH CREAMY BLUE CHEESE

1 head Iceberg Lettuce
1 Cup dried Cranberries
1 Cup Pecans or Walnuts, toasted and chopped

- Wash and dry the whole head of lettuce well.
- Cut lettuce into 4 wedges.
- Store wedges in the refrigerator covered with a damp
  paper towel until ready to serve.
- Place a lettuce wedge on a salad plate and top
  with desired amount of blue cheese dressing.
- Sprinkle with cranberries and nuts.

Makes 4 servings

CREAMY BLUE CHEESE DRESSING

1/2 Cup Mayonnaise
1/2 Cup Sour Cream
1/2 Cup Buttermilk
2 Tb grated Parmesan Cheese
1 tsp Worcestershire Sauce
1/2 tsp White Vinegar
1 Cup Blue Cheese, crumbled
Pinch of Sugar
Salt & Pepper, to taste

- In a medium bowl, whisk the mayonnaise, sour cream and buttermilk together until smooth.
- Stir in parmesan, Worcestershire, vinegar and sugar until well combined.
- Add blue cheese and season with salt & pepper.
- Cover and refrigerate for 1 hour.

Makes 2 cups

Roasted Asparagus Salad

ROASTED ASPARAGUS SALAD

1 Lb Asparagus, woody ends removed
1-2 Tb Extra Virgin Olive Oil
Salt & Pepper, to taste

1/4 Cup sliced Almonds, toasted
2 Oranges, peeled and sectioned
1/2 Cup Extra Virgin Olive Oil
1/4 Cup fresh Orange Juice
1 Tb Shallots, minced
1 tsp Dijon Mustard
1 tsp Honey
Salt & Pepper, to taste

- Preheat oven to 425 degrees.
- Place asparagus in a single row on a Silpat-lined, rimmed baking sheet.
- Drizzle with olive oil and sprinkle with salt & pepper.
- Roast the asparagus for 15–20 minutes, shaking pan every 5 minutes until spears
  are lightly charred and wilted.
- When asparagus is cool, angle cut into 1-inch pieces, reserving the tips.
- In a pitcher, rapidly whisk together the olive oil, orange juice, dijon, honey, shallots,
  salt & pepper until creamy.
- In a large bowl, toss the asparagus with the vinaigrette.
- Arrange the asparagus on a plate.
- Top with orange sections, toasted almonds and asparagus tips.
- Gently toss before serving.

Makes 4-6 servings

VARIATION:
- Replace Almonds with Pine Nuts
- Replace Orange slices with Sun-Dried Tomatoes
- Replace Orange Juice with Balsamic Vinegar
- Add 1/4 Cup Feta Cheese, crumbled
- Add 1 Tb fresh Basil, thinly sliced

FROM THE KITCHEN OF: HELEN SILVA

I have decided that Paula is the "essential ingredient" at Farmhouse Kitchen.

"SEE YOU WITH YOUR APRON ON"

MY LOVE OF APRONS STARTED AS A LITTLE GIRL. IN THE 1960'S IT WAS PART OF A WOMAN'S UNIFORM, AN EVER CHANGING "BADGE OF HONOR." YOUR HANDMADE APRON SILENTLY TOLD EVERYONE WHO YOU WERE AND WHAT SPECIAL MEAL YOU WOULD BE MAKING. IN MANY WAYS IT DEFINED YOU; THE COLOR, FABRIC, TRIM AND INTRICACIES ALL TOLD YOUR STORY. THE HOLIDAYS BROUGHT OUT THE PERFECTLY PRESSED APRONS WITH RED & GREEN "RICK-RACK." MY MOTHER WOULD ALWAYS TIE AN "EXTRA LARGE" APRON AROUND MY TINY BODY, SO AS NOT TO GET MY HOLIDAY DRESS SOILED. EVEN AS A CHILD, WEARING AN APRON MADE ME FEEL LIKE A BIG GIRL, LIKE I HAD JOINED THE SORORITY AND BEEN ACCEPTED INTO THE KITCHEN CLUB. THAT APRON GAVE ME PERMISSION TO COOK AND SO I DID. I WATCHED AND LISTENED INTENTLY, PICKING UP MORSELS OF KNOWLEDGE THAT I STILL USE TODAY. ALMOST LIKE A RITUAL, I REACH FOR MY APRON AS I ENTER THE KITCHEN. DEPENDING ON MY MOOD, AND OF COURSE THE SEASON, I MAKE AN APRON SELECTION. WHEN I TIE MY APRON IN THE FRONT I FEEL INSTANT COMFORT AND A FAMILIAR SECURITY. SO IT WILL COME AS NO SURPRISE THAT I LOVE CLOSING MY FARMHOUSE KITCHEN COOKING SCHOOL CORRESPONDENCE WITH: "SEE YOU WITH YOUR APRON ON!" YOU'LL ALWAYS FIND ME IN THE KITCHEN WITH MINE ON.

Rice, Grains & Beans

"NEVER LOOK BACK"

BEING A POTATO FARMER'S DAUGHTER YOU'D THINK I WOULD LOVE POTATOES. ON THE CONTRARY, HAVING BEEN SERVED SOME FORM OF POTATOES AT EVERY MEAL I HAPPILY REFRAIN. STARTING MY LOVE AFFAIR WITH RICE, GRAINS & BEANS WHEN I BECAME A VEGETARIAN IN COLLEGE, I NEVER LOOKED BACK. I FOUND COMPLETE SATISFACTION IN THE TEXTURE AND FLAVOR OF WHOLE GRAINS. THEY BECAME MY FLAVORFUL, FIBER-FILLED FRIENDS AND WERE THE FOUNDATION OF MY HEALTHY APPROACH TO COOKING. EATEN AS A STAPLE THROUGHOUT THE WORLD, RICE, GRAINS & BEANS ARE FINALLY "IN" AND FINDING THEIR WAY BACK INTO OUR SUPERMARKETS, PROVIDING THE PERFECT SCRUB-BRUSH FOR OUR FIBER-DEPRIVED SOCIETY. I ENCOURAGE YOU TO TAKE THE PLUNGE. YOU'LL NEVER LOOK BACK.

Coconut Basmati Rice 55, Citrus Couscous 57,
Wild Rice Salad 59,   Saffron Quinoa Pilaf 61, Greek Tabbouleh 63,
Wheat Berry Confetti Salad 65, White Bean & Tuna Salad 67,
Farmhouse Baked Beans 69

Coconut Basmati Rice

54

Coconut Basmati Rice

1 Cup white Basmati Rice
2 tsp unsalted Butter
2 whole Cloves
3 Black Peppercorns
1/4 Cup Scallion, sliced
3/4 Cup organic Chicken Stock
1/4 Cup unsweetened Coconut Milk
1/2 tsp Salt
2 Tb fresh Mint, chopped
2 Tb fresh Cilantro, chopped

- In a bowl, gently wash and drain the rice 4–5 times in lukewarm water (to remove the starch).
- Fill a bowl with fresh lukewarm water and soak the rice for 15 minutes.
- Drain rice and set aside.
- Melt butter in a medium saucepan.
- Add cloves and peppercorns, cook for 1 minute.
- Add rice and cook for 1–2 minutes, it will pop and sizzle!
- Add scallions and sauté for 1 minute.
- Add stock, coconut milk and salt.
- Bring to a gentle boil.
- Stir in rice and reduce heat to medium.
- Cover and simmer for 15 minutes or until the liquid is absorbed and the rice is tender.
- Remove from heat and place a paper towel on top of the rice, pressing gently.
- Replace cover and let the rice rest for 5 minutes.
- Fluff rice with a fork.
- Remove whole spices and stir in the mint and cilantro.
- Place rice in a decorative bowl and garnish with fresh cilantro leaves.

Makes 4-6 servings

CITRUS COUSCOUS

2 Cups fresh Orange Juice
1/2 Cup Water
1/2 tsp Salt
1- 10oz box Whole Wheat Couscous
1/2 Cup dried Apricots, sliced
1/2 Cup dried Currants
2 Tb Red Wine Vinegar
1 Cup seedless Cucumber, chopped
1/2 Cup Scallion, chopped
1/4 Cup Pine Nuts, toasted
1/4 Cup fresh Mint, chopped
1/4 Cup fresh Lemon Juice
2 Tb Extra Virgin Olive Oil
1 Orange, peeled and sectioned
Salt & Pepper, to taste
Scallion for garnish

- In a medium saucepan, bring 1 1/2 cups orange juice, water and salt to a boil.
- Gradually stir in couscous.
- Remove from the heat, cover and let stand for 5 minutes.
- Fluff with a fork and place in a large bowl.
- In a small saucepan, combine 1/2 cup orange juice, apricots, currants and vinegar.
- Bring mixture to a boil.
- Remove the dried fruit mixture from the heat and let stand for 15 minutes.
- Drain and discard the liquid.
- Add the dried fruit mixture, cucumbers, scallions, nuts, mint, lemon juice, oil and orange
  sections to the couscous.
- Season with salt & pepper and gently toss to combine.
- Place salad on a decorative platter and top with a scallion.

Makes 6-8 servings

Wild Rice Salad

WILD RICE SALAD

2 Cups Wild Rice Blend
4 Cups organic Chicken or Vegetable Stock
2 Tb unsalted Butter
1 small Yellow Onion, finely diced
1 Cup Scallion, finely sliced
1 Cup dried Cranberries
1 Cup Walnuts, toasted and chopped
1/2 tsp dried Thyme
1/4 Cup Extra Virgin Olive Oil
1 Tb roasted Walnut Oil (optional)
4 Tb Rice Wine Vinegar
1 Tb Honey Dijon Mustard
Salt & Pepper, to taste

- Rinse rice and let soak in a bowl of warm water for 15 minutes.
- Drain rice and set aside.
- In a medium saucepan, bring the chicken stock to a boil.
- Stir in rice blend and return to a boil.
- Reduce heat and simmer for 20–25 minutes.
- Rice should be "al dente."
- Place rice in a large bowl to cool, stirring occasionally.
- Melt the butter in a large skillet.
- Add the onions and sauté until they are soft and translucent.
- Stir into the rice the cooked onions, scallions, cranberries, walnuts and thyme.
- In a separate bowl, whisk together the oil, vinegar and mustard until creamy.
- Gently toss oil mixture into rice and season with salt & pepper.
- Place rice salad in a decorative bowl and serve at room temperature.

Makes 6-8 servings

SAFFRON QUINOA PILAF

2 1/2 Cups organic Chicken or Vegetable Stock
Pinch of Saffron
1 Tb Extra Virgin Olive Oil
1 small Yellow Onion, diced
1 clove Garlic, minced
1 Red Pepper, diced
1 1/2 Cups Quinoa
1/2 tsp Salt or to taste
Pinch of Cayenne Pepper

- Heat stock in a saucepan.
- Add saffron, stir and let sit for 15 minutes.
- In a heavy medium saucepan, heat oil on medium-high heat.
- Add onion, garlic and peppers and sauté until soft, about 5 minutes.
- Add quinoa, salt and cayenne and stir to coat quinoa well.
- Toast quinoa for 1–2 minutes, stirring frequently.
- Add saffron broth, stir once and then bring mixture to a boil.
- Cover and reduce heat to low and simmer for 5–10 minutes.
- Remove from heat and place a paper towel on top of the pilaf, pressing gently and replace lid.
- Replace cover and let the pilaf rest until ready to serve.
- When ready to serve, remove lid and paper towel, fluff pilaf with a fork.
- Place pilaf on a decorative platter and garnish with a few threads of saffron.

Makes 6 servings

Greek Tabbouleh

2/3 Cup Bulgur or Orzo
2 Cups Water
1 small Red Onion, finely chopped
1 tsp Salt
1/2 tsp Allspice
1/2 Cup fresh Mint leaves, finely chopped
1 Cup fresh Flat Leaf Parsley, finely chopped
1/2 Cup Scallion, finely chopped
1/4 Cup fresh Lemon Juice
1/4 Cup Extra Virgin Olive Oil
1 1/2 Cups seedless Cucumbers, finely chopped
1 1/2 Cups fresh Tomatoes, seeded and chopped
1 Cup canned Chickpeas, drained and rinsed
1/2 Cup crumbled Feta Cheese
1/2 Cup Black Olives, pitted and chopped
Salt & Pepper, to taste

ORZO TABBOULEH

- Place bulgur in a heatproof bowl.
- Bring water to a boil and pour over bulgur.
- Let bulgur rest, covered, for about 1 hour.
- Drain bulgur in a colander, pressing out any excess water.
- Return bulgur to large bowl and add all remaining ingredients.
- Toss well and season with salt & pepper.
- Refrigerate until ready to serve.

*If using orzo, cook in salted boiling water for 7–8 minutes, or until "al dente."
  Drain well.

Makes 6-8 servings

Wheat Berry Confetti Salad

WHEAT BERRY CONFETTI SALAD

1 1/2 Cups Wheat Berries
1 tsp Salt
1 Zucchini, cut into confetti
1 Carrot, cut into confetti
1 Red Pepper, cut into confetti
1 Yellow Pepper, cut into confetti
1 small Red Onion, cut into confetti
1/4 Cup Extra Virgin Olive Oil
3/4 Cup fresh Lemon Juice
1 tsp Salt
1/4 tsp Black Pepper
Pinch of Sugar

- Rinse the wheat berries and place in a heavy pot.
- Cover with 1-inch of water and add salt.
- Bring to a boil and simmer, uncovered, for 35–45 minutes or until wheat berries are soft and chewy.
- Drain wheat berries and place in a large bowl to cool, stirring occasionally.
- Stir all of the prepared vegetables into the wheat berries.
- In a small bowl, whisk together the oil, lemon juice, salt, pepper and sugar.
- Add the dressing to the wheat berry mixture and toss well.
- Adjust seasonings before serving.

*Soaking the berries overnight reduces cooking time!

WALDORF VARIATION:
- Replace the vegetables with 1 each Red, Green and Yellow Apple (skins on).
- Add 1/2 cup each toasted Walnuts, Raisins and Parsley.
- Replace the Lemon Juice with 1/4 Cup Cider Vinegar and 1/4 Cup Apple Juice.
- Add 1/4 tsp Cinnamon and pinch of Nutmeg.

Makes 6-8 servings

White Bean & Tuna Salad

WHITE BEAN & TUNA SALAD

1 bag dried Navy beans, cooked or 2 18oz cans White Cannellini Beans, drained and rinsed
1- 12oz can White Tuna in water, drained
1 small Red Onion, finely chopped
2 Tb Capers
1/2 Cup Currants
1/2 Cup Extra Virgin Olive Oil
1/4 Cup White Balsamic Vinegar
2-3 Tb Honey
2 Tb fresh Rosemary, chopped
Salt & Pepper, to taste
Fresh Rosemary for garnish

- In a large bowl, whisk together the oil, vinegar, honey,
  rosemary, salt and pepper until creamy.
- Add beans, tuna, onions, capers and currants, toss well and adjust seasonings.
- Spread bean mixture on a decorative platter and garnish with fresh rosemary.
- Serve with grilled bread.

*Fresh grilled Tuna can also be used with delicious results!

COOKING DRIED BEANS:

1 bag dried Beans
2 Cups Orange Juice
2 Cups organic Chicken Stock or Water
1 large Orange Peel
2 cloves Garlic
1 spring fresh Rosemary
2 Tb Extra Virgin Olive Oil, plus 2 Tb to add to cooked beans
1 tsp Salt
1/4 tsp Pepper

- Rinse dried beans and let them soak overnight in a large bowl of water.
- Drain and place in a large cast iron pot with remaining ingredients.
- Bring to a boil, lower the heat and simmer for 1 hour.
- Drain beans and cool in a large bowl, remove orange peel, garlic and rosemary.
- Toss with olive oil and adjust seasonings.

Makes 6-8 servings

Farmhouse Baked Beans

FARMHOUSE BAKED BEANS

1 Lb dried Navy or Great Northern Beans
1/2 Lb slab Bacon, cut into 1/4-inch pieces
1 large Yellow Onion, chopped
2 cloves Garlic, chopped
1 Cup Light Brown Sugar
2 Cups Ketchup
4 Tb Maple Syrup
4 Tb Molasses
2 Tb Worcestershire Sauce
1/2 tsp Salt, to taste
1/4 tsp Pepper

- Rinse and pick through the beans.
- Soak the beans overnight in a large bowl of water; they will soak up most of the water.
- Rinse the beans under cold water and place in a large cast iron pot.
- Cover with water and bring to a boil.
- Reduce heat and simmer for 45 minutes.
- Drain beans and reserve the cooking liquid.
- Preheat oven to 300 degrees.
- In a large cast iron pot, sauté the bacon until crisp and the fat is rendered.
- Add onions and garlic, continue to sauté until wilted, about 5 minutes.
- Add brown sugar and stir to dissolve.
- Add all the remaining ingredients along with the beans into the pot and mix well.
- Cover the pot and transfer to the oven.
- Bake, stirring occasionally for 2 1/2–3 hours making sure to scrape the bottom.
- Add reserved bean liquid as needed.
- Uncover and bake until sauce thickens, approximately 10–15 minutes longer.
- Serve hot.

*Baked Beans can also be made in a slow cooker.

Makes 10-12 servings

"COMPETING WITH YOGA"

MANY PEOPLE HAVE ASKED ME OVER THE YEARS WHY SO MANY PEOPLE COME TO FARMHOUSE KITCHEN COOKING SCHOOL. WEEK AFTER WEEK, YEAR AFTER YEAR, THE SAME FACES OFTEN REAPPEAR. MOST STUDENTS ARE AS COMFORTABLE IN THE FARMHOUSE KITCHEN AS THEY ARE IN THEIR OWN. I'VE COME TO REALIZE THAT IT'S NOT ABOUT THE FOOD. IT'S REALLY ABOUT THE LOVE YOU CAN ONLY FIND IN THE KITCHEN. I AM CONTINUALLY AMAZED AT HOW THE SIMPLE PROCESS OF COOKING AND SHARING A MEAL BRINGS THE SAME SERENITY YOU ACHIEVE WHEN PRACTICING YOGA. A COMMUNITY IS CREATED WITH THE SIMPLE INTENTION OF MAKING A MEAL. FOR A SHORT TIME THIS MAGICAL PROCESS ALLOWS EVERYONE TO FORGET AND LET GO OF ALL THEIR STRESS AND STRAIN. INSTEAD YOU SURRENDER TO THE COOKING PROCESS AND WITHOUT REALIZING IT YOU ARE LEFT WITH A FULL SPIRIT. MANY STUDENTS GO ON TO BECOME FRIENDS, MOST RETURN AGAIN AND AGAIN, NOT JUST FOR THE FOOD BUT ALSO FOR THE PEACE OF MIND THEY FIND THROUGH THE MAKING AND BREAKING OF BREAD.

I'D LIKE TO THANK MY STUDENTS FOR INSPIRING ME TO SHARE MY FAVORITE RECIPES AND REMINDING ME OF THE POWER OF FOOD.

Casseroles & One-Pots

"COMFORT FOOD NIRVANA"

TWENTY YEARS AGO MICHAEL AND I WERE GIVEN A CROCK POT AS A WEDDING GIFT, WHICH I IMMEDIATELY RETURNED! A MODERN WOMAN LIKE ME WOULDN'T BE CAUGHT DEAD USING A CROCK POT. THE NAME ALONE WAS UNBEARABLE. IN FULL DISCLOSURE, I WAS TRAUMATIZED AS A CHILD WITH A STEADY DIET OF ONE-POT MEALS. SOMEHOW THEY ALWAYS LOOKED AND TASTED THE SAME. SO I MADE A SILENT VOW THAT I WOULD NEVER SERVE MY FAMILY A ONE-POT MEAL. I'VE MADE A NEW VOW SINCE THEN AND MY CROCK POT, NOW FASHIONABLY CALLED A "SLOW COOKER" HAS BECOME A KITCHEN MUST-HAVE AND A LIFE-SAVING DEVICE. NOW TOUTED AS THE PATHWAY TO COMFORT FOOD NIRVANA, SLOW COOKING IS OFFICIALLY IN VOGUE. TRY IT AND YOU'LL FIND THAT THE LAYERING AND SLOW INFUSION OF FLAVOR CREATES A COMPLEXITY THAT LINGERS LONG AFTER THE MEAL IS DONE.

Farmhouse Beef Stew with Gremolata 73, Chicken Pot Pie 75, Seafood Paella 77, Moroccan Lamb Shank 79, Farmhouse Cassoulet 81, Coq au Vin Blanc 83, Black Bean Vegetable Chili with Cheddar Biscuits 85, Aunt Helen's Macaroni & Cheese 87, Chicken Casserole with Phyllo Roses 89

Farmhouse Beef Stew

FARMHOUSE BEEF STEW

3 Tb Extra Virgin Olive Oil or Canola Oil, (plus more as needed)
3 Lb boneless Beef Chuck, cut into 1-1/2 inch cubes
1/3 Cup Unbleached White Flour
1 tsp Orange zest
1 tsp dried Thyme
2 tsp Salt
1/2 tsp Pepper
2 medium Yellow Onions, chopped
3 cloves Garlic, minced
3 Celery stalks, chopped
1/2 tsp Cinnamon
2 Tb Tomato paste
2-inch Orange Peel
3 sprigs fresh Thyme or 1/2 tsp dried Thyme
2 Bay leaves
3 Cups Red Wine or Beef Stock or a combination of both
4 Cups Potatoes, peeled and cubed
6 Carrots, peeled and sliced
3 Tb fresh Flat Leaf Parsley, chopped

- Pat the beef dry with paper towels.
- Cut away any visible fat.
- In a large zip lock bag, place flour, zest, thyme, salt & pepper.
- Add the beef to the bag and shake to coat meat completely.
- In a heavy cast iron pot, heat 2 Tb of oil on medium-high heat.
- In batches, add 1/3 of the meat and brown all sides well,
  about 1–2 minutes each side.
- Set aside the browned meat in a bowl.
- Add 1 Tb of oil to the pot and reduce the heat to medium.
- Add the onions, garlic, celery and cinnamon.
- Cook until soft, stirring occasionally.
- Deglaze the pot with the tomato paste and stir for 1–2
  minutes with a wooden spoon to loosen the golden meat
  bits off the bottom of the pot, adding a little wine if necessary.
- Stir in the orange peel, herbs, meat and wine.
- Cover the pot and simmer, stirring occasionally,
  for 2–2 1/2 hours, or bake at 350 degrees
  for the same length of time.
- Add the potatoes and carrots.
- Simmer for an additional 20 minutes or until the
  vegetables are soft.
- Discard the orange peel, bay leaf and thyme sprigs.
- Serve stew over egg noodles.
- Sprinkle the top of the stew with fresh parsley or gremolata.

Makes 6-8 servings

GREMOLATA

1 Cup Flat Leaf Parsley,
  finely chopped
2 Tb Mint or Cilantro leaves,
  finely chopped
1-2 cloves Garlic, minced
1 Tb Orange or Lemon zest
2 tsp coarse Salt
Pinch of Red Pepper flakes
1 Tb Honey

- In a bowl or small food
  processor mix all ingredients
  together until combined.
- Chill in refrigerator until
  ready to use.
- A wonderful combination
  of flavors to sprinkle on top
  of stews, soups and tagine.

Makes 1 Cup

Chicken Pot Pie

CHICKEN POT PIE

SAUCE:
8 Tb unsalted Butter, (plus 1 Tb for dish)
8 Tb Unbleached White Flour
1 Cup organic Chicken Stock
2 Cups Half & Half
1/2 tsp Poultry Seasoning or dried Thyme
1/2 tsp Salt
1/4 tsp Pepper
1/2 Cup fresh Parsley, chopped

POACHED CHICKEN:
4 1/2-Lb organic, boneless, skinless
   Chicken Breasts
4 Cups organic Chicken Stock
1/2 Yellow Onion
1/2 tsp Peppercorns
2 sprigs of fresh Parsley

FILLING:
2 large Carrots, peeled & sliced
1 large Celery stalk, sliced
2 Potatoes, peeled & diced
1/2 Cup Corn kernels, fresh or frozen
1/2 Cup Peas (or Pea Pods), fresh or frozen
1/2 Cup Yellow Onion, chopped
2 Tb unsalted Butter
6 Mushrooms, sliced
1 clove Garlic, finely chopped
1 Sheet Puff Pastry Dough
1 large egg, lightly beaten with 2 Tb Milk,
   to brush on crust
Salt & Pepper, to taste

- Butter a large casserole dish.
- In medium saucepan, melt butter over
  medium heat.
- Stir in flour and cook for 1–2 minutes.
- Gradually add stock, whisking constantly.
- Whisk in half & half, herbs, salt & pepper.
- Continue to whisk and simmer until
  sauce thickens.
- Stir in fresh parsley and set sauce aside to cool.

- In a deep skillet, place chicken, stock,
  onion, fresh parsley and peppercorns.
- Bring to a boil and simmer chicken
  for about 20 minutes, or until a meat
  thermometer registers 165 degrees.
- Remove the chicken from the stock
  and strain the stock.
- Cool chicken and cut into 1/2-inch cubes,
  then set aside.

- Blanch all of the vegetables in reserved
  chicken stock except the mushrooms and
  garlic until fork tender.
- In a skillet melt 2 Tb of butter and
  sauté the mushrooms and garlic until golden.
- Do not stir the mushrooms for 2 minutes
  to encourage browning.

- In a large bowl combine the chicken,
  cream sauce, vegetables, and mushrooms.
- Preheat oven to 375 degrees.
- Place chicken mixture into the prepared
  casserole dish and cover with the puff pastry.
- Cut off excess pastry and use it to decorate
  the top of the pastry.
- Brush with egg and milk wash and sprinkle
  with salt & pepper.
- Bake for 30 minutes, or until crust is brown
  and filling is bubbling.

Makes 8 servings

Seafood Paella

SEAFOOD PAELLA

2 Lb firm White Fish (Cod, Haddock, Monk or Sea Bass), cut into 1-inch pieces
Salt & Pepper, to taste

1/4 Cup Spanish Olive Oil
1 large Yellow Onion, chopped
5 cloves Garlic, minced
1 tsp dried Oregano, plus 1/2 tsp to season fish
1/2 Lb Chorizo Sausage, or spicy-store bought Sausage,
  casings discarded and Sausage crumbled
1 Red Pepper, cut into thin strips
1 Green Pepper, cut into thin strips
1 large Tomato, chopped
2 Cups long grain Spanish Rice, rinsed under cold
  water and drained
4 Cups Clam or Seafood Stock
1 tsp Lemon zest
1/2 tsp Turmeric (optional) *intensifies yellow color
1/2 tsp Saffron, crumbled
1 tsp Salt, to taste
1 smoked Chipotle Pepper or 1/4 tsp Pepper or to taste
1/2 Lb Serrano Ham or Prosciutto, cut into thin strips
1/2 Lb small Clams, Mussels and Shrimp
2 Tb fresh Flat Leaf Parsley, chopped
Lemon wedges, for garnish

- Wash fish, pat dry and season with salt, pepper and 1/2 tsp oregano.
- Heat 3 Tb oil in a paella pan or large heavy skillet on medium-high heat.
- Add fish, stir for 4–5 minutes or until fish is nearly cooked.
- Remove fish and set aside in a bowl.
- Heat 3 additional tablespoons oil in the paella pan (leaving juice from cooked fish).
- Add the onion, garlic and the remaining 1 tsp oregano; stir and sauté until soft for 1–2 minutes.
- Add the chorizo or sausage and stir for 2–3 minutes.
- Add peppers, stir and sauté until soft.
- Add tomatoes and reduce heat to medium-low, simmering mixture for 10 minutes.
- Stir in rice, increase heat to medium and cook for 5 minutes.
- Add ham, zest, saffron, salt and chipotle pepper.
- Add stock and stir briefly. Do not stir after this point!
- Reduce the heat to medium-low and simmer for 18–20 minutes, or until all liquid has
  been absorbed and rice is tender; add more stock if needed.
- Re-add fish with clams and mussels.
- Cook paella for 10–15 more minutes, testing rice for tenderness.
- Increase heat to high for the last 1–2 minutes to encourage a browned bottom crust.
- Turn off heat and push the shrimp into the paella.
- Cover with foil and let rest for 5–10 minutes.
- Sprinkle with parsley and garnish with lemon wedges.
- Serve immediately in the paella pan.

Makes 8 servings

Moroccan Lamb Shank

MOROCCAN LAMB SHANK

1 Cup White or Navy Beans, rinsed and soaked overnight in water
3 Tb Extra Virgin Olive Oil, plus more as needed
2- 1-Lb Lamb Shanks
1/3 Cup Unbleached White Flour
2 tsp Salt
1 tsp Pepper
1 tsp Orange zest
1 large Yellow Onion, chopped
3 cloves Garlic, minced
3 Celery stalks, chopped
1/2 tsp each Allspice, Cinnamon and Cumin
2 Tb Honey
1- 2-inch Orange Peel
3 sprigs fresh Rosemary
3 Cups White Wine or Orange Juice or combination of both
1 Cup dried Apricots
4 Sweet Potatoes, peeled and cubed
4 Carrots, peeled and sliced
1/4 Cup golden Raisins
1/4 Cup sliced Almonds, toasted
2 Tb fresh Cilantro or Mint or a combination of both, chopped

- Pat lamb dry with paper towels.
- Cut away any visible fat.
- In a large ziplock bag, combine the flour, salt, pepper and zest.
- Place shanks in the bag, one at a time and shake to coat completely.
- In a heavy cast iron pot heat 2 tablespoons of oil on medium-high heat.
- Add the shanks to the pot and brown well on all sides.
- Remove shanks, set aside in a bowl.
- Add 1 Tb of oil to the pot and reduce heat to medium.
- Add onion, garlic and celery and cook until soft, stirring occasionally.
- Add the spices and cook 1–2 minutes.
- Deglaze the pot by adding honey to the vegetables and stirring for 1–2 minutes.
- Return the shanks to the pot and add wine, orange peel, drained beans and rosemary.
- Cover and simmer on medium-low heat, stirring occasionally, for 2 1/2 hours
  or bake at 350 degrees for the same amount of time.
- After 2 hours, add the apricots, potatoes and carrots and continue cooking for the remaining
  30 minutes or until the vegetables are soft.
- Discard rosemary sprigs and orange peel.
- Serve over couscous topped with raisins, almonds and fresh herbs.

Makes 6-8 servings

Farmhouse Cassoulet

FARMHOUSE CASSOULET

1 Tb Extra Virgin Olive Oil
1 medium Yellow Onion, chopped
2 cloves Garlic, minced
1- 15oz Can diced Tomatoes, drained
1 1/2 Cups organic Chicken Stock
1 Cup White Wine
2 Lb organic Chicken thighs, skin and fat removed
1 Lb Pork shoulder, trimmed and cut into 1-inch pieces
1 Tb Tomato Paste
2 sprigs fresh Thyme or 1/2 tsp dried Thyme
1 Bay leaf
1 Cup Panko Breadcrumbs
2- 18oz Cans Cannellini Beans, drained and rinsed
1/2 Lb Kielbasa, halved and cut into 1/2-inch pieces
1/2 tsp Salt
1/4 tsp Pepper
2 Tb unsalted Butter
1/4 cup fresh Parsley, finely chopped

- Wash chicken and pat dry with paper towels.
- Remove skin and cut away any visible fat.
- In a cast-iron pot, heat the oil on medium-high heat.
- Add onions and garlic, sauté until soft.
- Stir in tomatoes, stock, wine, chicken, pork, tomato paste, thyme and bay leaf.
- Cover the cassoulet and bring to a boil.
- Reduce heat to medium-low and simmer for 1 hour.
- Stir in 3/4 cup breadcrumbs, beans, kielbasa, salt and pepper.
- Remove and discard thyme sprigs and bay leaf.
- In a small skillet melt butter, add remaining 1/4 cup bread crumbs and parsley.
- Toss and toast crumbs for 3–4 minutes.
- Spoon cassoulet into individual bowls and sprinkle with toasted breadcrumb mixture.
- Serve with baguette.

Makes 6-8 servings

Coq au Vin Blanc

COQ AU VIN BLANC

3 Tb Extra Virgin Olive Oil, plus more as needed
3 Lb organic boneless, skinless Chicken (white and dark meat), cut into 1 1/2-inch cubes
1/2 Cup Unbleached White Flour
2 tsp Salt
1/2 tsp Pepper
1/2 tsp dried Thyme
Zest of 1 medium Lemon
1 large Yellow Onion, chopped
3 cloves Garlic, minced
1 medium Fennel bulb, cored and chopped
2 Cups assorted Mushrooms, sliced
1 Cup small canned or frozen Artichokes, halved
1 2-inch Lemon peel
1-2 Tb Capers
1/2 tsp dried Thyme or 2 sprigs fresh Thyme
2 Bay leaves
3 Cups White Wine
4 Cups Potatoes, peeled and quartered
2 Tb Heavy Cream
3 Tb fresh Flat Leaf Parsley, chopped
Salt & Pepper, to taste

- Wash the chicken and pat dry with paper towels.
- Cut away any visible fat.
- In a large ziplock bag add flour, salt, pepper, thyme and lemon zest.
- Add chicken and shake to coat meat completely.
- In a heavy cast-iron pot, heat 2 Tb of oil on medium-high heat.
- In batches, add 1/3 of the floured chicken to the pot, turning to brown all sides.
- Total cooking time is 5–7 minutes per batch.
- Set browned chicken aside in a bowl.
- Add an additional 1 Tb of oil to the pot and reduce heat to medium.
- Add onion, garlic, fennel and mushrooms to the pot and cook until vegetables are soft.
- Add 1/2 cup wine to deglaze the pot, scraping all of the golden bits off the bottom of the pot with a wooden spoon.
- Add artichokes, lemon peel, capers, herbs, chicken and remaining wine.
- Bring mixture to a boil.
- Cover and reduce heat to medium-low and simmer, stirring occasionally, for 1 hour, or bake at 350 degrees for the same amount of time.
- Add potatoes and simmer for an additional 20 minutes, or until potatoes are soft.
- Discard lemon peel, bay leaf and thyme sprigs.
- Using a slotted spoon, remove Coq au Vin from the pot and place in a large covered serving bowl.
- Add 2 Tb heavy cream to the sauce and simmer on high heat until reduced in half.
- Top the Coq au Vin with the reduced sauce.
- Sprinkle with fresh parsley.
- Serve with baguette.

Makes 6-8 servings

Black Bean Vegetable Chili

BLACK BEAN VEGETABLE CHILI

2 Tb Extra Virgin Olive Oil,
  (plus more to coat casserole dish)
1 large Yellow Onion, chopped
4 cloves Garlic, minced
1 Red Pepper, chopped
1 Yellow Pepper, chopped
1/2 fresh Jalapeno Pepper, seeded and finely
  chopped or to taste
1 Tb Chili Powder
1 tsp Cumin
1 tsp dried Oregano
1/2 tsp Coriander
1 Tb Semi-Sweet Chocolate Chips
1 Lime, juiced
1- 28oz Can whole Tomatoes, coarsely chopped
  with juice
2 medium Zucchini, cut into 1/2-inch cubes
1 Cup Corn kernels, fresh or frozen
2- 18oz Cans Black Beans, drained and rinsed
1 tsp Salt or to taste
1 Cup Pimento stuffed Olives, chopped (optional)
3 Tb fresh Cilantro, chopped
1 Recipe Cheddar Biscuits (optional)

- In a heavy cast-iron pot, heat oil on medium-
  high heat.
- Add onions and sauté until soft.
- Add garlic and peppers and sauté until wilted.
- Add spices and chocolate, stirring constantly
  for 1 minute.
- Add lime juice, tomatoes, zucchini and corn.
- Simmer partially covered, stirring occasionally,
  for about 20–30 minutes (if adding cheddar
  biscuits, reduce simmer time to 15 minutes).
- Stir in beans, olives, cilantro and salt.
- Transfer into a large oiled casserole dish.
- Chili can be served as is or topped with biscuit
  batter and baked.

Makes 6-8 servings

*For a milder chili, instead of using chopped jalapeno,
place entire jalapeno in the chili mixture while cooking.
Remove before serving.

CHEDDAR BISCUITS

1 Cup Unbleached White Flour
1 Cup Yellow Cornmeal
3/4 Cup Sharp Cheddar, grated
1 1/2 Tb Sugar
2 tsp Baking Powder
1/2 tsp Salt
1/2 tsp Cumin
1/4 Cup fresh Cilantro, chopped
1 tsp Jalapeno Pepper, seeded and finely
  chopped or to taste (optional)
3/4 Cup Buttermilk
3 Tb unsalted Butter, melted and cooled
1 large Egg, lightly beaten

- Preheat oven to 400 degrees.
- In a large bowl, whisk together flour,
  cornmeal, cheddar, baking powder, salt,
  cumin, cilantro and jalapeno.
- In a separate bowl whisk together
  buttermilk, butter and egg.
- Stir buttermilk mixture into flour mixture
  and blend until just combined.
- Drop batter by large spoonfuls (about 8)
  over chili, spacing them evenly.
- Bake in the middle of the oven for 10 minutes.
- Reduce temperature to 350 degrees and
  bake chili until topping is cooked through
  and chili is bubbling, about 30 minutes.

AUNT HELEN'S MACARONI & CHEESE

BREADCRUMBS:
1 Cup Panko Breadcrumbs
1/4 Cup Parmesan Cheese, grated
1/4 tsp Salt
1/8 tsp Pepper
2 Tb unsalted Butter, melted

CHEESE:
1 Cup Jarlsberg or Swiss Cheese, grated
3/4 Cup Parmesan Cheese, grated
1 Cup Cheddar Cheese, grated

MACARONI:
1 Lb Penne Pasta
1 Tb Salt

CREAM SAUCE:
2 Tb unsalted Butter
2 tsp Unbleached White Flour or Wondra
1 1/2 Cups Heavy Cream
1/4 tsp Salt and 1/4 tsp White Pepper
Fresh grated Nutmeg, to taste

- Preheat oven to 425 degrees.
- In a small bowl, combine all of the ingredients for the breadcrumbs and set aside.
- Combine cheeses in a large bowl and set aside.
- In a large pot, bring 4 quarts of water to a rolling boil.
- Add salt and pasta, stir and cook until very "al dente."
- Drain pasta in a colander, leaving the penne slightly wet.
- Add the HOT pasta to the bowl of cheese.
- While pasta is cooking, melt butter in a medium saucepan, whisk in flour until smooth and cook for 2 minutes.
- Gradually whisk in cream in a steady stream.
- On medium heat, whisk and simmer until cream sauce thickens, 2–3 minutes.
- Add salt, pepper and nutmeg.
- IMMEDIATELY pour cream sauce over the pasta.
- Cover the bowl with foil and let mixture rest for about 3 minutes.
- Do Not Stir!
- After 3 minutes, uncover and stir with spatula until cheeses are melted and mixture is well combined.
- Transfer pasta to a buttered 13" x 9" baking dish.
- Sprinkle with breadcrumbs, pressing down lightly.
- Bake until top is golden brown, about 7–10 minutes.
- Serve immediately or can be made a day ahead and baked before serving.

Makes 6-8 servings

CHICKEN CASSEROLE WITH PHYLLO ROSES

CHICKEN:
2 1-Lb organic boneless, skinless Chicken Breasts
1 tsp Salt
1/2 tsp Pepper
2 Tb Extra Virgin Olive Oil, (plus more to coat casserole dish)
1 medium Red Onion, thinly sliced
2 cloves Garlic, chopped
1/2 tsp Allspice

ORZO:
1 Cup Orzo
4 Cups organic Chicken Stock

FILLING:
1 1/2 Cups plain whole milk Greek Yogurt
1/2 Cup fresh Flat Leaf Parsley, finely chopped
1/2 Cup Scallion, finely chopped
1 tsp Lemon zest
1 1/2 Cups fresh Tomatoes, seeded and chopped
1 Cup canned Chickpeas, drained and rinsed
1/2 Cup Feta Cheese, crumbled
1/2 Cup Black Olives, pitted and chopped
Salt & Pepper, to taste

PHYLLO:
6-12 Sheets Phyllo Dough, thawed
4 Tb unsalted Butter, melted

- Preheat oven to 400 degrees.
- Generously oil a large casserole dish.
- Wash and pat chicken dry, cut into 1-inch cubes.
- Season with salt & pepper.
- In a skillet, heat oil and sauté chicken until golden brown, about 7–10 minutes.
- Transfer chicken to a plate to cool slightly.
- In the same skillet, add the onion, garlic and allspice.
- Sauté until soft.
- In a medium pot, bring chicken stock to a boil, add orzo and stir.
- Gently boil for 5–6 minutes, uncovered or until orzo is "al dente."

- Drain well and place orzo in a large bowl to cool to room temperature, toss with a little olive oil.
- Add all filling ingredients and the chicken to the cooked orzo.
- Toss and lightly season with salt & pepper.
- Transfer to the prepared casserole dish.
- Butter one layer of phyllo dough, fold it in thirds lengthwise, then roll end to end, making a rose.
- Place on top of the casserole.
- Repeat with the remaining sheets of phyllo until the casserole is completely covered.
- Brush the top of the phyllo roses with melted butter.
- Bake until casserole is golden and bubbling, 25–30 minutes.

Makes 6-8 servings

"FOOD IS LOVE"

MY HUSBAND MICHAEL OFTEN ASKS ME WHY I NEVER SIT DOWN WHEN WE'RE EATING. I REMIND HIM OF ONE OF MY MOST TREASURED CHILDHOOD MEMORIES: SEEING MY POLISH GRANDMOTHERS STANDING IN THEIR KITCHEN DOORWAYS, WITH THEIR FLAVOR-LADEN APRONS, AND A SATISFIED SMILE ON THEIR FACES. THEY NEVER SAT DOWN DURING A MEAL AND WE WERE TOO BUSY EATING OUR SECOND OR THIRD HELPINGS TO NOTICE THAT "BABCHI" WAS NOT AT THE TABLE. HER PLEASURE CAME FROM REFILLING ANOTHER PLATTER WITH STEAMING HOT FOOD AND WATCHING HER LOVED ONES ENJOY. WHEN I ASKED HER WHY SHE NEVER SAT DOWN ALL SHE REPLIED WAS "FOOD IS LOVE." MY MOTHER AND NOW I TOO UNDERSTAND THAT THERE IS NO GREATER PLEASURE THAN SHARING GOOD FOOD WITH THE ONES YOU LOVE.

Meats & Seafood

"AN EDIBLE SPONGE"

NEVER BEING A TRUE CARNIVORE, I'VE ALWAYS TAKEN A FLAVOR-FILLED APPROACH TO COOKING MEATS & SEAFOOD. I TREAT THEM AS AN EDIBLE SPONGE, READY AND WILLING TO TAKE IN THE FLAVOR CHOICES OF THE COOK. THE FINEST RESULTS COME FROM CHOOSING THE FRESHEST, MOST NATURAL CUTS AND USING A SIMPLE PREPARATION. I'VE LEARNED HOW TO CREATE A MASTERFUL MAIN COURSE FROM MEATS & SEAFOOD BY COAXING IN FLAVORS, WHEREIN THE "SPONGE" BECOMES THE MEAL'S MASTERPIECE.

Stuffed Chicken Breast with Red Grape Puree and Swiss Chard 93,
Thai Turkey Burger with Wasabi Mayonnaise 95, Honey Sage Pork Chops and Potato Pancakes 97,
Rosemary Chicken and Spinach Gratin 99, Southern Barbecue Ribs 101,
Glazed Asian Salmon with Mint and Lime Tartar Sauce 103, Mussels in Coconut Curry Sauce 105,
Poached Fish with Fennel and Apples 107, Grilled Garlic Shrimp and Orange Salsa 109,
Citrus Scallops on Rosemary Skewers 111

Stuffed Chicken Breast With Red Grape Puree

Swiss Chard

92

STUFFED CHICKEN BREAST WITH RED GRAPE PUREE

2 Cups Red seedless Grapes
1-2 Tb Extra Virgin Olive Oil,
  (plus more to drizzle on chicken)
Salt & Pepper, to taste
2- 1-Lb organic boneless, skinless Chicken Breasts,
  cut in half
1 Cup Feta, Brie or Gorgonzola, crumbled
1/2 Cup Pine Nuts, Pecans or Walnuts, toasted
1 Cup Red Grapes, chopped
1/2 Cup White Wine
2 Tb fresh Parsley, Cilantro or Mint, chopped

- Preheat oven to 450 degrees.
- Place the 2 cups of grapes on a Silpat-lined
  rimmed baking sheet.
- Drizzle with olive oil and sprinkle with
  salt & pepper.
- Roast in the oven until grapes soften and
  caramelize, about 10–15 minutes.
- Shake the pan and roll the grapes
  every 5 minutes.
- Take the grapes out of the oven and set
  aside to cool.
- Lower oven temperature to 350 degrees.
- Line a 9"x 13" pan with foil and lightly oil.
- Cut chicken breasts in half and make a
  "pocket" in one side of each, about 3/4 of
  the way through.
- Season the chicken with salt & pepper.
- In a bowl mix together the cheese, chopped
  nuts and grapes.
- Stuff each pocket of chicken with the
  cheese mixture.
- Place chicken breasts in the prepared pan
  and add the white wine.
- Season with salt & pepper, drizzle with olive oil.
- Bake for 30–40 minutes, or until the chicken
  registers 165 degrees using a meat thermometer.
- Remove chicken from the oven and cover with foil.
- Place roasted grapes in a deep bowl.
- Using a hand blender, puree the roasted
  grapes until smooth.
- Place the chicken on a plate and top each
  piece with grape puree.
- Sprinkle with fresh herbs.

Makes 4 servings

SWISS CHARD

1/2 Cup Currants
1 Tb Balsamic Vinegar
3 Tb Extra Virgin Olive Oil
1 small Yellow Onion, finely chopped
2 cloves Garlic, minced
1 bunch Swiss Chard
1 Cup organic Chicken Stock
2 Tb Honey
4 Tb Pine Nuts, toasted
1/4 Cup Pimento stuffed Olives, finely chopped
Salt & Pepper, to taste
Lemon wedges, for garnish

- In a small bowl soak currants in vinegar.
- In a large skillet, heat oil on medium-high heat.
- Add the onion and garlic, sauté until soft.
- Rinse and finely chop chard, including
  stems, creating a ribbon effect.
- Add chard and chicken stock to the skillet.
- Cover and sauté on medium-high heat for
  10 minutes, or until soft.
- Mix currants, vinegar, honey, nuts and olives
  into the chard.
- Season with salt & pepper.
- Sauté uncovered until the liquid has
  evaporated and the chard is tender.
- Garnish with lemon wedges and serve.

Makes 4-6 servings

Thai Turkey Burger

THAI TURKEY BURGER

1 Lb ground Turkey
2 Scallions or 1/4 Cup Red Onions, finely chopped
1/4 Cup Soy Sauce
3 Tb fresh Parsley or Cilantro
1/2 tsp fresh Ginger, peeled and grated
    or 1/4 tsp ground Ginger
1/8 tsp Red Pepper flakes
1 each seedless Cucumber, Yellow and Red Pepper

- In a bowl, gently mix all of the ingredients with the turkey.
- Using an ice cream scoop to measure, form turkey
  into patties.
- Grill on lightly oiled grill racks, 2–3 minutes each side,
  or until meat thermometer inserted in the center of the
  burger reads 165 degrees.
- Serve in a toasted pita with matchstick cucumber, yellow and red pepper
  tossed in Asian vinaigrette.
- Top with wasabi mayonnaise.

WASABI MAYONNAISE
1/2 Cup Mayonnaise
3 Tb Scallions, finely sliced
2 tsp fresh Ginger, peeled and grated or 1 tsp ground Ginger
2 tsp Soy Sauce
1 tsp Wasabi Paste or Powder

- In a small bowl, blend all ingredients together until smooth.
- Keep covered in refrigerator for up to 1 week.

ASIAN VINAIGRETTE
1/4 Cup Canola Oil
1 Tb roasted Sesame Oil
2 Tb Rice Wine Vinegar
1/2 tsp fresh Ginger, grated or 1/4 tsp powdered Ginger
1 tsp Sugar
Salt & Red Pepper flakes, to taste

- Place oils in a pitcher and rapidly whisk in vinegar, ginger, sugar,
  salt & pepper until creamy.

Makes 6 burgers

HONEY SAGE PORK CHOPS

4- 1/2 Lb boneless Pork Chops
1 tsp Dijon Mustard
2 Tb Honey
1 Tb fresh Sage leaves, chopped
4 cloves Garlic, minced
Pinch of Cayenne Pepper
Salt, to taste

- In a ziplock bag, mix together all
  marinade ingredients.
- Add pork chops to the bag and marinate
  for 1–3 hours in the refrigerator.
- Sear, grill, bake or roast the pork chops until
  the internal temperature reaches 155 degrees.
- Top with Caramel Apples, (Page 135)
  and serve with potato pancakes.

Makes 4 servings

POTATO PANCAKES

Potato Pancakes

2 Cups raw Potatoes, peeled and grated
2 Tb Unbleached White Flour
2 large Eggs, lightly beaten
1 Tb Yellow Onion, grated
1 tsp Salt
1 tsp Sugar
Canola Oil, to coat griddle
Applesauce and Sour Cream, to garnish

- In a bowl, let the grated potatoes soak in cold water until ready to make the batter.
- Drain and blot potatoes dry with paper towels.
- In a bowl mix the potatoes, flour, eggs, onion, salt and sugar until combined.
- Preheat and generously oil the griddle on medium-high heat.
- Drop spoonfuls of batter, spreading as thinly as possible, onto the griddle.
- Cook pancakes on each side for 3–4 minutes.
- Allow the pancakes to brown well before flipping.
- Serve with warm applesauce and sour cream.

Makes 10-12 pancakes

Rosemary Chicken

ROSEMARY CHICKEN

8 organic Chicken drumsticks, skin attached
1 Tb unsalted Butter
1 Tb fresh Rosemary leaves
3 Tb Maple Syrup
2 tsp Cider Vinegar
Salt & Pepper, to taste

- Preheat oven to 450 degrees.
- Line a shallow baking pan with foil.
- Rinse the chicken and pat dry.
- Generously season chicken with salt
  and pepper.
- Arrange chicken, skin side down, in
  the pan and bake for 10 minutes.
- While the chicken is baking, combine the
  butter, rosemary and maple syrup in a small
  saucepan.
- Simmer mixture, stirring occasionally, for
  about 1–2 minutes.
- Take the mixture off the heat and stir
  in the vinegar.
- Lower the oven to 350 degrees.
- Turn the chicken drumsticks over and spoon
  half of the rosemary mixture onto the chicken.
- Bake 10 minutes longer then spoon on
  remaining glaze.
- Continue baking the chicken for 10–15
  minutes, spooning on glaze, until the
  chicken is golden brown and registers
  165 degrees using a meat thermometer.
- Transfer chicken to a plate, spoon on pan
  juices and garnish with fresh rosemary.

Makes 4 servings

SPINACH GRATIN

1/2 Lb Mushrooms, cleaned and chopped
2 Tb unsalted Butter
2 cloves Garlic, finely chopped
2- 10oz packages frozen or fresh Spinach
   (thawed, cooked, drained and patted dry)
2 large Eggs, lightly beaten
1- 15oz container Ricotta Cheese
1/2 Cup plus 1 Tb grated Parmesan Cheese
1/2 tsp Salt
1/4 tsp Pepper
Pinch of fresh Nutmeg
2 Tb Panko Bread Crumbs

- Preheat oven to 375 degrees.
- Butter a 2-quart casserole dish.
- In a large skillet, melt butter and sauté
  garlic and mushrooms over medium-high
  heat until soft, about 5 minutes.
- Don't stir mushrooms for the first 3 minutes!
- Remove mushrooms from heat to cool.
- Place mushrooms in large bowl and stir in
  spinach, eggs, ricotta, parmesan, salt, pepper
  and nutmeg.
- Spoon the spinach mixture into the
  prepared casserole dish.
- In a small bowl, mix breadcrumbs with 1 Tb
  parmesan and sprinkle on top of spinach mixture.
- Gratin can be made in the morning, covered
  and refrigerated until ready to bake.
- Bake for 35 minutes or until bubbling and
  crust is golden brown.

Makes 6 servings

Southern Barbecue Ribs

SOUTHERN BARBECUE RIBS

3 Lb Pork Spareribs
1 Tb Canola Oil
1 medium Yellow Onion, chopped
2 cloves Garlic, minced
1/2 Cup White Vinegar
1/2 Cup Water
1/4 Cup Ketchup or Chili Sauce
2 Tb Lemon Juice
2 Tb Worcestershire sauce
3 Tb Light Brown Sugar
1 1/2 tsp Salt
1 tsp dried Mustard

- Preheat oven to 450 degrees.
- Bake ribs on a Silpat or foil-lined rimmed sheet pan for 30–40 minutes.
- While the ribs are baking, in a saucepan heat the oil, adding the onion and garlic and sauté
  until soft.
- Stir in the remaining ingredients and simmer for 10 minutes.
- After the sauce is finished, generously baste both sides of the ribs with the sauce.
- Bake the ribs for an additional 10–15 minutes per side.
- Cut ribs between each bone and serve with remaining barbecue sauce and Farmhouse Baked
  Beans (page 69).

Makes 6 servings

FROM THE KITCHEN OF: MONIQUE STANTON

It is a gift to be able to educate others about your passion. Paula possesses that gift.

Glazed Asian Salmon

GLAZED ASIAN SALMON

4- 6oz Salmon Strips
3 Tb Maple Syrup
2 Tb Rice Wine Vinegar
1 Tb Hoison Sauce
1 tsp Sesame Oil

- Combine all of the marinade ingredients
  in a bowl, setting aside 1-2 tablespoons.
- Using a paper towel, lightly oil grill racks
  before starting grill.
- Grill salmon, uncovered, on medium-high
   heat for 3 minutes.
- Turn and brush fish with marinade and
  grill for an additional 3 minutes.
- Turn and brush with remaining marinade.
- Grill 2–3 minutes longer, or until fish
  flakes easily with a fork.
- Place salmon on a platter and drizzle
  with the reserved marinade.
- Serve with cucumber salsa, top with
  mint and lime tartar sauce.

CUCUMBER & FRESH HERB SALSA

1 seedless Cucumber, diced into 1/4-inch cubes
1 tsp each Cilantro, Parsley, Dill and Chive
Juice of a Lime
1 tsp Salt
Pinch of Sugar or drizzle of Honey

- Combine all ingredients in a bowl and toss.
- Chill until ready to use.

Makes 4 servings

MINT & LIME TARTAR SAUCE

1 Cup Mayonnaise
1/4 Cup Red Onion, finely chopped
1/4 Cup Golden Raisins, coarsely chopped
2 Tb Light Brown Sugar
1/4 tsp Coriander
1/4 Cup Dill Pickles, chopped
2 Tb Capers, drained and chopped
1 Tb fresh Lime Juice
1 tsp Jalapeno Pepper, seeded and finely
   chopped or to taste
1/2 Cup fresh Mint and/or Cilantro, chopped

- In a bowl, stir together all ingredients.
- Chill until ready to serve.

* Delicious with all seafood!

Mussels In Coconut Curry Sauce

MUSSELS IN COCONUT CURRY SAUCE

3 Tb Canola Oil
1 medium Yellow Onion, chopped
2 cloves Garlic, finely chopped
1 Tb fresh Ginger, grated
1 tsp Curry Powder
2 1/2 Cups unsweetened Coconut Milk
2 Lb cleaned Mussels
Salt and Red Pepper flakes, to taste
Fresh Cilantro, chopped, for garnish

- In a large bowl, soak the cleaned mussels in ice cold water with 1 tablespoon salt for 1 hour.
- In a covered large skillet, heat the oil.
- Add onion and garlic, sauté until golden.
- Add ginger, curry powder and a generous pinch of salt and red pepper flakes.
- Stir for 1 minute.
- Add coconut milk to skillet and bring to a boil.
- Drain the mussels and add to the simmering coconut milk.
- Cover and cook the mussels over medium heat, for about 5 minutes, or until the mussels have just opened.
- Discard any mussels that have not opened.
- Transfer the mussels and poaching liquid into a large serving bowl.
- Sprinkle with cilantro and serve immediately.

*Any fish can be cooked in the same manner!

Makes 6 servings

4- 8oz White Fish Fillets
   (Cod, Flounder, Haddock, Sole or Tilapia)
2 sprigs fresh Tarragon
1 tart Green Apple, cored and thinly sliced with skin on
1 Fennel bulb, cored and thinly sliced
1/2 Cup fresh Lime Juice or White Wine
1/4 Cup Rice Wine Vinegar
4 Tb frozen Apple Concentrate, thawed
4 tsp Soy Sauce
1 Scallion, finely chopped, for garnish
2 Tb fresh Dill, Mint, Parsley and/or Cilantro, finely
   chopped, for garnish
4 Lime Wedges, for garnish

- In a covered large skillet, layer the apples, fennel and tarragon.
- Top with fish, being careful not to let the fillets overlap.
- In a bowl, whisk together lime juice, vinegar, apple concentrate and soy sauce.
- Pour mixture over the fish.
- Poach the fish over medium-high heat for 6–8 minutes, or until the fish flakes
  easily with a fork.
- Keep skillet covered while cooking.
- Place the apples and fennel in soup bowls and top with the fish fillets
  and pan juices.
- Sprinkle with scallions and fresh herbs and garnish with lime wedges.

Makes 4 servings

Grilled Garlic Shrimp

Orange Salsa

GRILLED GARLIC SHRIMP

3 cloves Garlic, smashed
1 tsp coarse Salt
Juice of 1 Lime
1/4 Cup Orange Marmalade
2 Tb fresh Cilantro, chopped
4 Tb Olive Oil
1 Tb Soy Sauce
1/4 tsp Red Pepper flakes, to taste
1 Lb (24) medium Shrimp, peeled, de-veined, with tails
Fresh Cilantro, for garnish
6 Bamboo skewers, soaked in water 30 minutes

- Smash garlic with salt, making a paste.
- In a bowl whisk together garlic paste, lime
  juice, marmalade, cilantro, 3 tablespoons oil, soy
  sauce and red pepper flakes.
- Put aside 1/3 of the marinade to use as a
  dipping sauce.
- In a ziplock bag combine the shrimp with
  the remaining marinade.
- Marinate shrimp in the refrigerator for 15
  minutes, turning bag once.
- Drain shrimp, pat dry and thread onto skewers.
- Place the shrimp skewers on a lightly oiled grill
  or skillet on high heat.
- Grill without turning until the shrimp
  are crusted and curl on one side, then
  turn and crust on the other side.
- Total cooking time is 3 minutes.
- Transfer to a warm dish and sprinkle
  with cilantro.
- Serve immediately with orange salsa and
  dipping sauce.

ORANGE SALSA

2 Oranges, peeled, sectioned and chopped
1/4 Cup Red Onion, chopped
1 Tb Jalapeno Pepper, seeded and finely
  chopped or to taste
1 Tb Honey
Salt & Pepper, to taste

- In a bowl, combine all ingredients
  and mix well.
- Chill until ready to serve.

Makes 4-6 servings

Makes 2 Cups

Citrus Scallops On Rosemary Skewers

CITRUS SCALLOPS ON ROSEMARY SKEWERS

1 Lb Sea Scallops
1/4 Cup Cointreau or Grand Marnier
Zest of 1 Orange
1 Tb Light Brown Sugar
1 Tb fresh Rosemary, chopped
2 Tb unsalted Butter, melted
6 long fresh Rosemary stems
2 large Oranges, sliced

- In a ziplock bag, mix all the marinade ingredients.
- Add the scallops and marinate in the refrigerator for
  at least 1 hour, or until ready to grill.
- Remove 3/4 of the leaves from the top of the rosemary stems.
- Thread one side of orange slice, a scallop, then the other side of
  the orange lengthwise on the rosemary stems.
- Using a paper towel, lightly oil the grill rack before starting grill.
- Place a 2-inch wide strip of aluminum foil on the front of the grill.
- Lay rosemary leaves on the foil and the scallops on the grill.
- Grill scallops until you can see that the scallop is cooked a little
  more than half way up the side, about 1–2 minutes.
- Using a spatula, carefully turn and continue grilling the second
  side for about 1–2 minutes longer.
- Serve immediately.

Makes 4 servings

"THE MORE BUTTER THE BETTER"

MY STUDENTS OFTEN ASK HOW I LEARNED TO COOK. THE ANSWER IS SIMPLY THAT I GREW UP IN A POLISH KITCHEN. YOU SEE I HAD TWO POLISH GRANDMOTHERS: "BABCHI" MARKISZ AND "BABCHI" SKWARA. ONE AN ELEGANT COOK TRAINED IN DENMARK, THE OTHER A POTATO FARMER'S WIFE WHO BELIEVED "THE MORE BUTTER THE BETTER!" BEING A FARMER'S DAUGHTER BOTH OF MY PARENTS WORKED IN THE FIELDS, SO MY DAYCARE WAS IN "BABCHI" SKWARA'S KITCHEN. AS A CHILD I COULDN'T WAIT TO BE DROPPED OFF AND SEE WHAT WE'D BE COOKING THAT DAY. A POLISH WOMAN'S FIRST THOUGHT IN THE MORNING WAS ALWAYS, "WHAT WILL I FEED THE MEN?" I WOULD GET TO "BABCHI'S" KITCHEN EARLY IN THE MORNING. USUALLY SHE WAS ALREADY MAKING THE DOUGH FOR THE PIEROGI'S OR SAUTÉING THE ONIONS FOR CHEESE AND POTATO FILLING. IN NO TIME SHE WOULD ROLL OUT A HUGE RING OF DOUGH ON THE HEAVILY FLOURED GREY FORMICA KITCHEN TABLE AND GIVE ME AN EMPTY SAUERKRAUT CAN TO CUT CIRCLES OF DOUGH. SHE SHOWED ME HOW TO PLACE A TABLESPOON OF POTATO FILLING IN THE CENTER OF EACH DOUGH PILLOW SO WE COULD PINCH THE PIEROGI CLOSED. I'M SURE SHE NEVER KNEW HOW HONORED I WAS TO BE HER ASSISTANT. HOLIDAYS WERE SPENT IN HOLYOKE, MASSACHUSETTS, WITH "BABCHI" AND DZIADZIA MARKISZ. BEING BROUGHT UP IN DENMARK THIS "BABCHI" WAS VERY "LADY-LIKE." SHE ALWAYS WORE A DRESS AND HER CRYSTAL NECK-LACE WHEN COOKING IN THE KITCHEN. I WAS IMPRESSED WITH HER STYLE, WHICH SHE CARRIED INTO HER ARTFUL COOKING. HER COOKING WAS CLEAN AND REFINED, THE INGREDIENTS CAREFULLY SELECTED AND SIMPLY PREPARED. SHE NEVER MASKED THE FRESHNESS OF A DISH WITH TOO MUCH BUTTER OR SALT. THE TABLE WAS ALWAYS CAREFULLY SET, WITH A FLORAL CENTERPIECE AND CLOTH NAPKINS. LITTLE DID SHE KNOW THAT I WATCHED HER EVERY MOVE AND THAT I THINK OF HER TO THIS DAY EVERY TIME I PUT ON HER CRYSTAL BEADS. THESE WOMEN WERE MY TEACHERS AND THEIR FINGERPRINTS ARE ALL OVER THESE RECIPES. MY HOPE IS THAT YOU WILL LEARN AS MUCH FROM THEM AS I DID.

Desserts

"LASTING IMPRESSION"

THERE ISN'T ANYTHING MORE INTOXICATING TO ME
THAN THE SCENT OF FRESHLY BAKED COOKIES. THE WAFTING
GOODNESS TAKES ME STRAIGHT BACK TO MY CHILDHOOD. SO
I'LL CONFESS RIGHT AWAY: I PREFER DESSERT TO ALMOST
ANY MAIN COURSE. I OFTEN PREPARE IT FIRST AND
PROUDLY DISPLAY IT ON A PEDESTAL FOR EVERYONE TO
ADMIRE. IT'S THE ULTIMATE TEMPTATION, LEAVING A
LASTING IMPRESSION AND DREAMS OF WANTING MORE.

Blackberry Jam Cupcakes 115, Espresso Kahlua Brownies 117, Lemon Squares 119,
Blueberry Crumb Tart 121, Jane's Apple Cake 123, Chocolate Truffles 125,
Farmhouse Apple Crisp 127, Very Berry Cobbler 129, Outrageous Cookies 131

Blackberry Jam Cupcakes

BLACKBERRY JAM CUPCAKES

3 Cups Unbleached White Flour
1 1/4 tsp Salt
1 1/2 tsp Allspice
1 1/2 tsp Clove
1/2 tsp Cinnamon
1 Cup (2 sticks) unsalted Butter, softened
2 Cups Sugar
5 large Eggs, lightly beaten
1 Cup Buttermilk, well shaken
1 tsp Baking Soda
1 Cup seedless Blackberry Jam
Fresh Blackberries, for garnish

- Preheat oven to 350 degrees.
- Place paper liners in cupcake tins.
- On wax paper, sift together flour, salt and spices.
- In a measuring cup, stir together buttermilk and baking soda.
- In the bowl with an electric mixer cream butter and sugar until light and fluffy.
- Add eggs, one at a time, beating well after each addition.
- In 3 separate alternating batches, add the flour then buttermilk to the butter mixture on low speed.
- Add jam to the batter and mix until just combined.
- Using an ice cream scoop fill prepared cupcake tins with batter 3/4-full.
- Bake in the middle of the oven for 20–25 minutes for standard cupcakes,
  (10–15 minutes for mini cupcakes), or until toothpick inserted in center comes out clean.
- Cool cupcakes, then using a teaspoon, drizzle with warm caramel icing and top with
  a fresh blackberry.

Makes 24 large cupcakes or 48 mini cupcakes

GRAMMY'S CARAMEL ICING OR PENUCHE

1/2 Cup (1 stick) unsalted Butter
1 Cup Light Brown Sugar
1/4 Cup Whole Milk
1 3/4 Cups Confectioners Sugar, sifted

- Melt butter in a medium saucepan.
- Add brown sugar and bring to a boil over medium heat, stirring constantly with a whisk.
- While continuing to whisk, carefully stir in milk and bring it back up to a boil.
- Icing will bubble when milk is added!
- Cool on the countertop to lukewarm, then using a whisk, gradually add confectioners sugar.
- Whisk rapidly until icing is thick enough to spread.
* If icing becomes too stiff, add a little hot water.

Makes 2 cups

Espresso Kahlua Brownies

ESPRESSO KAHLUA BROWNIES

1/2 Cup (1 stick) unsalted Butter, softened
 (plus 1 Tb for pan)
3 oz unsweetened Chocolate, chopped
1 1/4 Cups Sugar
2 large Eggs, lightly beaten
1 tsp Vanilla Extract
3 Tb instant Espresso Powder
2 Tb Kahlua
3/4 Cup Unbleached White Flour
1/2 tsp Baking Powder
1/4 tsp Salt

- Preheat oven to 350 degrees.
- Line a 9" x 9" baking pan with aluminum foil, leaving a 2-inch overhang, and butter well.
- Melt the butter and chocolate over a double boiler (stainless steel bowl set over a saucepan
  with 1-inch of simmering water).
- Let cool on the counter.
- In a medium bowl, blend together eggs, sugar, vanilla, espresso powder and kahlua.
- Blend the melted chocolate mixture into the egg mixture.
- In a separate bowl, whisk together flour, baking powder and salt.
- Fold into the chocolate mixture, mixing until just combined.
- Do not over mix!
- Spread batter evenly into the prepared pan.
- Bake in the middle of the oven for 25–30 minutes, or until a toothpick inserted comes out clean.
- Do not over bake!
- Lift foil with baked brownies from the pan.
- Cool brownies on a metal rack for 10 minutes.
- Gently peel foil off the brownies and place them on a cutting board.
- Cut into squares with a plastic knife.
- Serve slightly warm or at room temperature.

Makes 12 Brownies

Lemon Squares

LEMON SQUARES

SHORTBREAD:

1/2 Cup unsalted Butter, room temperature
  (plus 1 Tb for pan)
1 Cup Unbleached White Flour
1/4 Cup Confectioners Sugar, sifted
Pinch of Salt

- Preheat oven to 350 degrees.
- Line a 9" x 9" baking pan with aluminum foil, leaving
  a 2-inch overhang. Butter well.
- In a food processor, cream together all ingredients until
  they form a ball.
- Press dough into the bottom of the prepared pan.
- Bake for 20 minutes, or until light brown.
- While the crust is baking, prepare the lemon curd.

LEMON CURD:

2 large Eggs, lightly beaten
1 Cup Sugar
1/4 tsp Salt
Juice and Zest of 1 Lemon
1/4 Cup Unbleached White Flour
1/2 tsp Baking Powder

- In a bowl, using an electric mixer, beat eggs well gradually adding in the sugar.
- While mixing slowly, add the remaining ingredients.
- Reduce oven to 325 degrees.
- Immediately pour topping over hot shortbread and return to oven.
- Bake for 30–35 minutes, or until top is lightly golden.
- Lift foil with baked lemon squares from the pan.
- Cool on a metal rack for 20 minutes.
- Gently peel foil off the lemon squares and place them on a cutting board.
- Cut into squares with a plastic knife.
- Sprinkle with confectioners sugar.

Makes 12 squares

Blueberry Crumb Tart

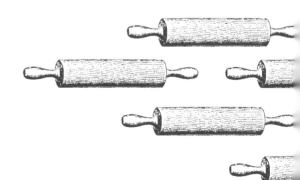

BLUEBERRY CRUMB TART

2 Cups fresh or frozen Blueberries
1/4 Cup Blueberry Jam
1- 9-inch Pie Crust
Butter Crumb Topping, recipe below

- Preheat oven to 425 degrees.
- Place pie crust on a Silpat-lined, unrimmed cookie sheet, and crimp crust edges.
- Spread jam on crust and top with blueberries.
- Sprinkle on crumb topping.
- Bake for 30 minutes, or until the crust and topping is golden.
- Immediately slide the tart off of the Silpat onto a metal rack using a large angled knife or spatula.

Makes 6-8 servings

FLAKY PIE CRUST

4 Cups Unbleached White Flour
1 Tb Sugar
1 tsp Salt
1 3/4 Cups Vegetable Shortening
1/2 Cup Cold Water
1 Tb White Vinegar
1 large Egg, lightly beaten

- In a food processor combine flour, sugar and salt.
- Add shortening and pulse until mixture resembles crumbs.
- In a measuring cup, mix the water, vinegar and egg together.
- With the food processor running, pour in the egg mixture and continue to blend until dough forms a ball.
- Divide dough into 4 pieces, flatten and wrap with wax paper.
- Chill for at least 1 hour, or for best results overnight.
- Let dough warm on the counter for 5–10 minutes, then roll out between two pieces of lightly floured wax paper.

Makes 4, 8-inch pie crusts or 3, 9-inch pie crusts.

BUTTER CRUMB TOPPING

1/2 Cup cold, unsalted Butter, cut into 1/2-inch pieces
1 Cup Unbleached White Flour
3/4 Cup Sugar

- In a bowl, mix together flour and sugar.
- Place butter pieces on top of the flour mixture.
- Using a pastry blender, cut butter into the flour mixture until crumbs form.

Makes 2 cups

Jane's Apple Cake

JANE'S APPLE CAKE

1 1/2 Cups Canola Oil
2 Cups Sugar
3 large Eggs, lightly beaten
1 tsp Vanilla Extract
3 Cups Unbleached White Flour (plus 1 Tb for pan)
1 tsp Cinnamon
1 tsp Salt
1 tsp Baking Soda
3 Cups Apples, peeled and sliced
1 Cup Raisins or dried Cranberries
1 Cup Walnuts, toasted and chopped

- Preheat oven to 350 degrees.
- Butter and flour a tube pan.
- With an electric mixer, combine the oil and sugar in a bowl.
- Add eggs and vanilla to the sugar mixture, blending until combined.
- On a sheet of wax paper sift together the flour, cinnamon, salt and baking soda.
- Add the flour mixture to the batter and mix until just combined.
- Do not over mix!
- Add apples, dried fruit and nuts to the batter and mix until just combined.
- Evenly spread the batter into the prepared pan
- Bake the cake in the center of the oven for 1 hour, or until toothpick inserted comes
  out clean.
- Cool cake on a wire rack before removing from the pan.

Makes 10-12 servings

FROM THE KITCHEN OF: LISA SANNINO

You are our very own "Martha Stewart" of the North Fork.

Chocolate Truffles

CHOCOLATE TRUFFLES

1 Cup Heavy Cream
2 oz unsalted Butter
20 oz (1 lb 4 oz) Semi-Sweet, Milk and/or Bittersweet Chocolate
1-2 Tb Extract or Spirits or Spice
   (Vanilla Extract, Grand Marnier, Espresso powder,
   Chili powder, Curry, Paprika)
Unsweetened Cocoa powder, Nuts, Coconut,
   to coat truffles

- Chop chocolate and place in a stainless steel bowl.
- Combine cream and butter in a heavy saucepan.
- Bring the cream mixture to a simmer. Do not boil!
- Remove from the heat and pour cream mixture over the chopped chocolate.
- Let the milk and chocolate mixture rest for 1–2 minutes, then stir until
  chocolate is melted and smooth.
- Let mixture cool on the counter until tepid then stir in extract, spirits or spice.
- Cool uncovered in the refrigerator until mixture becomes firm.
- Using a tiny ice cream scoop, create balls of truffle mixture.
- Roll each ball between your palms to make perfectly round truffles.
- Then roll in unsweetened cocoa powder, chopped nuts or toasted coconut.
- Keep in a covered container in the refrigerator or in a cool place.

Makes 50 truffles

Farmhouse Apple Crisp

FARMHOUSE APPLE CRISP

FRUIT FILLING:
4 Cups mixed Apples, peeled and thinly sliced
1/2 Cup Sugar
2 Tb Unbleached White Flour
1/2 tsp Cinnamon or 1 tsp Lemon or Orange Zest

CRUMB TOPPING:
1/2 Cup (1 stick) cold unsalted Butter, cut into 1/2-inch
pieces
1/2 Cup Unbleached White Flour
3/4 Cup Light Brown Sugar
1 Cup Old-Fashioned Oatmeal

- Preheat oven to 375 degrees.
- In a medium bowl, mix apples, sugar, flour and cinnamon or zest.
- Place fruit mixture in a buttered casserole dish.
- In a separate bowl, mix together the flour and brown sugar.
- Place the cold butter pieces on top of the flour mixture.
- Using a pastry blender, cut butter into the flour mixture until it forms crumbs.
- Combine the butter crumbs with the oatmeal.
- Top the apples with the crumb topping.
- Place the casserole dish on a Silpat-lined rimmed baking sheet.
- Bake for 40–50 minutes or until bubbling and golden.
- Serve warm with honey-sweetened Greek yogurt or vanilla ice cream.

Makes 6-8 servings

VARIATIONS:
- Use any fruit in season!
- Add 1/2 cup Pecans, Walnuts or Coconut to the crumb mixture.

FROM THE KITCHEN OF: CATHERINE HARPER
*Paula's kitchen is truly
a magical place.*

VERY BERRY COBBLER

BERRY FILLING:

4-5 Cups mixed fresh seasonal Berries (Strawberries should be quartered)
1 Tb fresh Lemon Juice
1/2 Cup Sugar
2 Tb Unbleached White Flour or Cornstarch (plus 1 Tb if using Strawberries)
1/2 tsp Cinnamon or pinch of fresh Nutmeg
1 tsp Lemon or Orange Zest (optional)

- Preheat oven to 375 degrees.
- Butter an ovenproof casserole dish.
- In a medium bowl mix together berries, lemon juice, sugar, flour and spices.
- Place mixture in the prepared dish.

COBBLER TOPPING:

1 Cup Unbleached White Flour
1/4 Cup plus 2 Tb Sugar
2 tsp Baking Powder
1/2 tsp Salt
1/2 tsp Cinnamon
3 Tb cold unsalted Butter, cut into 1/2-inch pieces
1/2 Cup Buttermilk
1 large Egg, lightly beaten
1 tsp Lemon or Orange zest

- In a medium bowl, combine flour, 1/4 cup sugar, baking powder, salt and cinnamon.
- Cut butter into the flour mixture with a pastry blender until it resembles crumbs.
- In a separate bowl, mix buttermilk, egg and zest together.
- Add buttermilk mixture to the flour mixture and mix until just combined.
- Do not over mix!
- Dollop spoonfuls of batter evenly on top of the fruit.
- Sprinkle with 2 tablespoons of sugar.
- Place the casserole dish on a Silpat-lined rimmed baking sheet.
- Bake for 40–50 minutes or until bubbling and golden.

Makes 6 servings

OUTRAGEOUS COOKIES

1 Cup (2 sticks) unsalted Butter, softened
1 Cup Sugar
1 Cup Light Brown Sugar
2 large Eggs, lightly beaten
2 Tb Water
1 tsp Vanilla Extract
2 Cups Unbleached White Flour
1 tsp Baking Soda
1 tsp Salt
2 Cups Quick-Cooking Oatmeal
2 Cups Semi-Sweet Chocolate Chips
1 Cup Toffee Bits
1 Cup Walnuts, toasted and coarsely chopped
1 1/2 Cups dried Cranberries

- Preheat oven to 375 degrees.
- With an electric mixer, cream butter and sugars on medium speed until
  light and fluffy in a bowl.
- Add the eggs, water and vanilla to the butter mixture and blend until smooth, 1–2 minutes.
- In a separate bowl, combine flour, baking soda and salt.
- With mixer on low speed, gradually blend flour mixture into liquids until just combined.
- Do not over mix!
- Fold in remaining ingredients.
- Drop a tablespoon of dough onto a Silpat- or parchment-lined unrimmed cookie sheet
  3 inches apart.
- Bake for 10–12 minutes, or until cookies are golden brown.
- Remove cookies from cookie sheets and cool on a metal rack.

Makes 5 dozen cookies

"COMING FULL CIRCLE"

I'D LIKE TO THINK THAT I'VE COME FULL CIRCLE. GROWING UP I WAS INSTILLED WITH AN APPRECIATION OF WHAT THE EARTH PROVIDES. COOKING AND BAKING WAS WOVEN INTO THE FIBER OF MY CHILDHOOD. IT'S SO NATURAL FOR ME TO SHARE THE SECRETS OF MY KITCHEN, RECREATING THE LOVING ENVIRONMENT THAT MY GRANDMOTHERS RAISED ME IN. SO I CONSIDER MYSELF A COUNTRY COOK. GENUINELY APPRECIATING THE TREASURES OF THE SEASONS, EAGER TO SHARE MY FARM-TO-TABLE APPROACH TO COOKING.

Breakfast & Breads

"YOU CAN'T MISS"

BRUNCH HAS ALWAYS BEEN MY FAVORITE MEAL TO PREPARE FOR FAMILY AND FRIENDS. IT'S THE IN-BETWEEN MEAL THAT HAS NO RULES. NOT REALLY BREAKFAST OR LUNCH, IT FREES YOU FROM A PRE-DETERMINED MENU. FOR ME IT'S A SIMPLE FEAST, EASILY PREPARED, MEANT FOR SAVORING OVER GOOD CONVERSATION. IT'S THE MEAL NO ONE WANTS TO MISS!

Oatmeal Pancakes with Caramel Apples 135,
Stuffed Croissant French Toast with Maple Blueberry Compote 137,
Farmhouse Buttermilk Biscuits with Lemon Curd 139,
English Currant Scones with Flavored Butters 141, Irish Soda Bread 143,
Cheese Babka 145, Corny Corn Bread 147, Banana Chocolate Chip Bread 149

Oatmeal Pancakes

Caramel Apples

Oatmeal Pancakes

2 Cups Old-Fashioned Oatmeal
1/2 Cup Unbleached White Flour
1/3 Cup Sugar
1 tsp Baking Powder
1 tsp Baking Soda
2 Cups Buttermilk
2 large Eggs, lightly beaten
1 tsp Vanilla Extract
   or Lemon zest or Orange zest or Cinnamon
1 Cup Mini Chocolate Chips (optional)
   or sliced Apple, Peach or Berries (optional)
1 Tb Butter plus 1 Tb Vegetable Oil, melted to coat griddle

- In a large bowl, combine all dry ingredients.
- In a measuring cup, whisk together buttermilk, eggs
  and vanilla.
- Mix wet and dry ingredients together until just combined.
- Let batter sit at room temperature at least 1 hour, or best chilled overnight.
- Heat griddle over medium-high heat.
- Brush lightly with melted butter-oil mixture.
- Using an ice cream scoop for measuring, drop 1/4 cup or 1 scoop of batter,
  evenly spaced, onto griddle.
- Cook, flipping only once, for approximately 2–3 minutes on each side, or until golden.
- Serve immediately or cover with foil and keep warm in a 200-degree oven.
- Sprinkle with powdered sugar.
- Serve with warm maple syrup or caramel apples.

Makes 12 pancakes

Caramel Apples

1 Cup Light Brown Sugar
1/2 Cup unsalted Butter
1/2 tsp Cinnamon
3 Apples, peeled and thinly sliced

- In a metal skillet, melt butter on medium-high heat.
- Add brown sugar and stir until dissolved.
- Stir sliced apples and cinnamon into the sugar mixture.
- Continue cooking on high until fruit is tender and mixture is caramelized.
*Delicious topping for pancakes or French toast!

Makes 3 cups

Stuffed Croissant French Toast

STUFFED CROISSANT FRENCH TOAST

1 Cup Half & Half
4 large Eggs, lightly beaten
2 Tb Sugar
2 tsp Vanilla Extract
1/4 tsp Salt
1- 8 oz package Cream Cheese or Mascarpone, softened
1/4 Cup Blueberry Jam or other fruit jam
6 Croissants
1 Tb Butter plus 1 Tb Canola Oil, melted to coat griddle

Maple Blueberry Compote

- In a shallow bowl, whisk the eggs, half & half, sugar, vanilla and salt together.
- In a small bowl, blend cream cheese and jam until combined.
- Cut croissants almost completely in half.
- Spread each croissant with 1 Tb of cream cheese mixture.
- Gently soak and turn croissants in egg mixture until saturated.
- Heat griddle over medium-high heat.
- Brush lightly with butter-oil mixture.
- Place the croissants on griddle and cook until underside is golden brown, approximately 2–3 minutes.
- Gently flip and cook the second side until golden.
- Serve immediately or cover with foil and keep warm in a 200-degree oven.
- Sprinkle with powdered sugar or top with maple blueberry compote.

Makes 6 Croissants

MAPLE BLUEBERRY COMPOTE

1 Cup fresh or frozen Blueberries
1 Cup Maple Syrup
1/2 tsp Cinnamon
1 Cup toasted Pecans, chopped

- Place the berries, syrup, cinnamon and pecans into a metal skillet.
- Simmer the mixture on medium-high heat until berries soften, approximately 4–5 minutes.
- Serve with French toast or pancakes!

Makes 3 cups

Farmhouse Buttermilk Biscuits

Lemon Curd

BISCUIT VARIATIONS:

- Lemon: Add 1 tsp Lemon Zest instead of Vanilla Extract to Buttermilk
- Chocolate: Add 1/3 Cup unsweetened Cocoa Powder and
  1/2 Cup mini, Semi-Sweet Chocolate Chips to flour mixture.
- Coconut: Add 1 1/2 Cups toasted sweetened Coconut to flour mixture.

BUTTERMILK BISCUITS

2 Cups Unbleached White Flour
1/3 Cup Sugar
1 1/2 tsp Baking Powder
3/4 tsp Baking Soda
8 Tb cold, unsalted Butter,
  cut into 1/2-inch pieces
3/4 Cup Buttermilk
1/2 tsp Vanilla Extract
1 Tb Milk plus 1 Tb Sugar for milk wash

- Preheat oven to 400 degrees.
- In a medium-size bowl, mix together all
  dry ingredients.
- Place cold butter pieces on top of the
  flour mixture.
- With a pastry blender cut butter into flour
  mixture until it resembles coarse crumbs.
- Add buttermilk and vanilla to flour
  mixture and stir until just combined.
- Move dough onto a floured surface and
  gently knead for 30 seconds or until
  dough just comes together.
- With a lightly floured rolling pin roll
  dough out into a 1/2-inch thick circle.
- Cut the dough with a floured 2-inch
  biscuit cutter and evenly space on a
  Silpat-lined, unrimmed baking sheet.
- Brush biscuits with milk and sprinkle
  with sugar.
- Bake 10–12 minutes or until just golden.
- Cool biscuits on a metal rack.
- When cool, cut in half and top with
  lemon curd and a strawberry slice.

Makes 24 biscuits

LEMON CURD

1/2 Cup unsalted Butter
3/4 Cup Sugar
1/2 Cup fresh Lemon Juice
2 Tb Lemon zest
Pinch of Salt
6 Egg Yolks, lightly beaten

- Melt butter in a heavy saucepan over
  medium heat.
- Remove pan from the heat and whisk in
  sugar, lemon juice, lemon zest and salt.
- Whisk in egg yolks until smooth.
- Return pan to medium heat and cook,
  whisking constantly until mixture thickens,
  approximately 4–5 minutes.
- Do not let the mixture boil!
- Check consistency by dipping a wooden spoon
  into the curd and drawing your finger across
  the back of the spoon. Your finger should
  leave a path and no curd should run down
  the spoon.
- Immediately force curd through a fine sieve.
- Cool to room temperature, whisking
  occasionally.
- Refrigerate covered.

Makes 2 cups

English Currant Scones

ENGLISH CURRANT SCONES

2 Cups Unbleached White Flour
1/3 Cup Sugar
1 1/2 tsp Baking Powder
1/2 tsp Baking Soda
1/4 tsp Salt
8 Tb cold, unsalted Butter, cut into 1/2-inch pieces
1/2 Cup Buttermilk
1 large Egg, lightly beaten
1 1/2 tsp Vanilla Extract
2/3 Cup Currants
1 Tb Milk plus 1 Egg, lightly beaten, for egg wash

- Preheat oven to 400 degrees.
- In a medium-size bowl, stir together all of the dry ingredients.
- Place cold butter pieces on top of flour mixture.
- With a pastry blender cut butter into the flour mixture until it resembles coarse crumbs.
- Add buttermilk, egg, vanilla and currants and mix until just combined.
- Move dough onto a lightly floured surface and gently knead for 30 seconds or
  until dough just comes together.
- With a lightly floured rolling pin, roll out dough into a 1/2-inch thick circle.
- Cut dough with a floured 2-inch biscuit cutter and evenly space on a Silpat-lined,
  unrimmed baking sheet.
- Brush scones with the egg wash.
- Bake 10–12 minutes, or until just golden.
- Serve warm with flavored butters.

VARIATIONS:
Chocolate Chip: 2/3 cup mini, Semi-Sweet Chocolate Chips instead of Currants.
Orange: 1 tsp Orange Zest instead of Vanilla Extract.

Makes 24 biscuits

FLAVORED BUTTERS
Add to 1 stick softened, unsalted butter:
- 1 tsp Orange or Lemon Zest plus 1 Tb Honey or
- 1/4 tsp Cinnamon plus 1 Tb Honey or
- 1 Tb fresh Mint, finely chopped plus 1 Tb Honey

FROM THE KITCHEN OF: CARLA DAVIS
This is not a mere cooking class it's a life experience.

Irish Soda Bread

IRISH SODA BREAD

4 Cups Unbleached White Flour (plus 1 Tb for dusting)
1/2 Cup Sugar
2 tsp Baking Powder
1 tsp Baking Soda
3/4 tsp Salt
3 Cups assorted dried Fruit
   (Yellow Raisins, Cranberries, Currants, Cherries and/or Blueberries)
1 Tb Caraway Seeds (optional)
2 eggs, lightly beaten
1 1/4 Cups Buttermilk
1 Cup Sour Cream

- Preheat oven to 350 degrees.
- Butter a 9-inch round pan, or (4) 6-inch pans.
- In a large bowl, combine all dry ingredients.
- In a separate bowl blend eggs, buttermilk and sour cream.
- Stir egg mixture into flour mixture until just combined.
- Dough will be very sticky.
- Transfer dough to prepared pan(s) and dust with flour.
- Bake large bread for 50–60 minutes, smaller breads for 30–40 minutes, or
  until toothpick inserted comes out clean.
- Cool in pans for 10 minutes, and then transfer to a wire rack.

Makes 1 large bread or 4 small breads

FROM THE KITCHEN OF:
PETER & SANDRA BARSCZESKI
We've learned to expand our
horizons at Farmhouse Kitchen.

Cheese Babka

Cheese Babka

Dough:
1 Cup Sour Cream
1/2 Cup Sugar
1/2 Cup unsalted Butter, melted
2 Eggs, lightly beaten
2 packages Dry Yeast
1/2 Cup warm Water, 110 degrees
4 Cups Unbleached White Flour
1 tsp Salt (add last, do not let touch yeast!)

Filling:
2 - 8oz packages Cream Cheese, softened
3/4 Cup Sugar
1 Egg, beaten
1/8 tsp Salt
2 tsp Vanilla Extract

Glaze: (optional)
2 Cups Confectioners Sugar, sifted
4 Tb Milk
2 tsp Vanilla

- In a saucepan, heat the sour cream, sugar and butter on medium heat.
- Stir and cook until butter melts and ingredients are well combined.
- Remove from the heat and cool to lukewarm, then add eggs.
- Sprinkle yeast over warm water in a warmed glass jar, stirring to dissolve.
- Let rest for 5 minutes.
- In a large bowl combine dissolved yeast, sour cream mixture, flour and salt.
- Using a spatula, mix the dough until well combined.
- Place in a lightly oiled container with a lid and refrigerate overnight.
- Prepare filling by blending the cream cheese and sugar in a bowl until well combined.
- Add the egg, salt and vanilla and stir until smooth and creamy.
- Divide dough into 4 parts.
- On a well floured surface, roll each dough into a 12" x 18" rectangle.
- Spread 1/4 of filling on each rectangle to 1/2-inch from the edge.
- Roll up like a jelly roll lengthwise.
- Seal edges and fold them under to seal-in cheese mixture.
- Place babka, seam side down, on a Silpat-lined baking sheet (2 babka per baking sheet).
- Cover with lightly oiled plastic wrap or a damp kitchen towel and allow to rise
  in a warm place until doubled in size, about 1 hour.
- Bake at 375 degrees for 15 minutes, or until lightly browned.
- Prepare glaze by blending the sugar, milk and vanilla in a bowl until smooth.
- Spread babka with glaze while still warm.
- Babka freezes beautifully.

Makes 4 babka

Corny Corn Bread

CORNY CORN BREAD

2 Cups Whole Milk
1 Cup Canola Oil
5 Eggs, lightly beaten
1 Cup Sugar
3 1/2 Cups Unbleached White Flour
1 1/3 Cups Cornmeal
2 Tb Baking Powder
1 tsp Salt
3 Cups Corn kernels, fresh or frozen
   (If using frozen corn rinse under hot water for 1 minute
   and drain well)

- Preheat oven to 350 degrees.
- Butter a 12" x 18" rimmed baking pan.
- In a large bowl, combine sugar with milk, oil and eggs.
- In a medium bowl, stir together the flour, cornmeal, baking powder and salt.
- Add dry ingredients to liquid mixture and stir until just combined.
- Stir in corn.
- Pour batter into the prepared pan.
- Bake for 30–40 minutes, or until toothpick inserted comes out clean.
- Cool in the pan, then cut in squares and serve.

Makes 12 squares

SAVORY CORN BREAD
- Decrease the Sugar to 1/4 cup and add 1/2 cup chopped fresh Cilantro
  and 1 tsp finely chopped Jalapeno pepper to the batter.
- Serve with Jalapeno butter.

JALAPENO BUTTER
Add to 1 stick softened, unsalted butter:
- 1 tsp finely chopped Jalapeno pepper plus 2 Tb Honey plus a pinch of Salt.
- Blend until combined.
- Place Jalapeno butter in a ramekin and refrigerate until ready to serve.

Banana Chocolate Chip Bread

BANANA CHOCOLATE CHIP BREAD

2 Cups Unbleached White Flour
1 tsp Baking Powder
1/2 tsp Baking Soda
1/2 tsp Salt
1/2 Cup unsalted Butter, softened
1 Cup Sugar
2 Eggs, lightly beaten
1 1/4 Cups mashed ripe Banana (approximately 2 bananas)
1 tsp Vanilla Extract
1 Cup Mini Semi-Sweet Chocolate Chips
1 Cup Walnuts, toasted and chopped (optional)

- Preheat oven to 350 degrees.
- Butter 1 large or 8 mini bread pans.
- In a bowl, combine all dry ingredients.
- In a separate large bowl, cream butter and sugar together.
- Add eggs, banana and vanilla and stir until combined.
- Add the dry ingredients and mix until just combined.
- Fold in chocolate chips and walnuts.
- Pour batter into the prepared pans.
- Bake mini breads for 20–30 minutes, large bread for 50–60 minutes or until toothpick
  inserted comes out clean.
- Cool in pan(s) for 10 minutes.
- Transfer bread(s) from pan(s) to a wire rack and continue to cool.

Makes 1 large bread or 8 mini breads

FROM THE KITCHEN OF: KAREN PAULICK

Being in Paula's kitchen
is about sharing the love
that goes into cooking.

"IN MY PANTRY"

BAKING:	Baking Soda, Baking Powder, Cornmeal, Pure Vanilla Extract, Espresso Powder, Old Fashioned Oatmeal, Sweetened Flaked Coconut, Toffee Chips, Yeast (Fast Rising)
BEANS:	Canned (Black, Red Kidney, Garbanzo, Cannellini) Dried (Cannellini or Navy Bean)
BREAD:	Croissant, French Baguette, Kaiser Rolls
CHOCOLATE:	Bittersweet, Semi-sweet, Un-sweetened Bar, Semi-Sweet Chocolate Chips
CONDIMENTS:	French Dijon Mustard, Hoisin Sauce, Mayonnaise, Soy Sauce, Wasabi Powder, Worcestershire Sauce
DRIED FRUIT:	Apricots, Blueberries, Cherries, Cranberries, Currants, White Raisins
DRIED HERBS:	Bay leaves, Oregano, Thyme
DRIED SEEDS:	Caraway Seeds, Fennel Seeds
DRIED SPICES:	Allspice, Cinnamon, Clove, Coriander, Cumin, Curry, Fresh Nutmeg, Saffron, Turmeric
FLOUR:	Unbleached All Purpose, Whole Wheat, Wondra
JAMS:	French-Blueberry, Marmalade, Peach, Raspberry
MISC:	Capers, Dill Pickles, Green Olives, Kalamata Olives, Panko Bread Crumbs, Unsweetened Coconut Milk, Vegetable Shortening
LIQUORS:	Grand Marnier, Kahlua
NUTS:	Pecans, Pine Nuts, Sliced Almonds, Walnuts
OILS:	Canola, Extra Virgin-Cold Pressed Olive, Roasted Walnut, Roasted Sesame, Spanish Olive
PASTA:	Orzo, Penne, Whole Wheat
PEPPERS:	Cayenne, Fresh Cracked Black, Peppercorns, Red Pepper Flakes, Smoked Chipotle Peppers
RICE:	Arborio, Basmati, Jasmine, White Spanish, Whole Wheat Long Grain, Wild
SALT:	Coarse, French Sea Salt, Fine Iodized Salt
STOCK:	(Organic) Beef, Chicken and Vegetable
SUGAR:	Confectioners, Light Brown, Local Honey, Maple Syrup, Molasses, White Granular
TOMATOES:	(Organic) Canned Crushed and Chopped with Onions, Ketchup, Paste (in a tube), Sun-dried (not in oil)
VINEGAR:	Balsamic, Cider, Rice Wine, White Wine, Red Wine
WHOLE GRAINS:	Bulgur, Couscous, Quinoa, Wheat-Berries

"IN MY REFRIGERATOR"

CHEESE:	Brie, Cheddar, Chevre, Feta, Mozzarella, Parmigiano Reggiano, Roquefort
DAIRY:	(Organic) Buttermilk, Cream Cheese, Large Brown Eggs, Greek Yogurt, Half & Half, Heavy Cream, Milk, Sour Cream, Unsalted Butter
FRESH HERBS:	Basil, Cilantro, Dill, Flat-Leaf Parsley, Mint, Rosemary, Tarragon, Thyme, Sage
FROZEN:	Apple Concentrate, Artichokes, Baby Peas, Corn, Phyllo Dough, Puff Pastry
FRUIT:	(Organic) Green, Red, Yellow Apples, Bananas, Blackberries, Blueberries, Green, Red Grapes, Lemon, Lime, Orange, Pink Grapefruit, Raspberries, Strawberries
JUICES:	(Organic) Cranberry, Orange, Guave, Mango
MEAT:	Bacon, Chorizo, (Free Range and Grass Fed) Beef, Pork and Lamb, Kielbasa, Serrano Ham
POULTRY:	(Organic) Chicken, Ground Turkey
SEAFOOD:	(Local) Clams, Mussels, Salmon, Sea Scallops, White Fish
VEGETABLES:	(Organic) Baby Arugula, Asparagus, Carrots, Celery, Cucumbers (seedless), Eggplant, Fennel, Garlic, Ginger Root, Iceberg, Mache, Romaine, Spinach Greens , Leek, Mushrooms, Baby Red, White, Yukon Gold North Fork Potatoes, Red, Yellow Onions , Green, Jalapeno, Red, Yellow Peppers, Scallions, Swiss Chard (multicolor), Tomatoes

"YOU'RE MY FAVORITE"

I WOULD BE LYING TO SAY I DON'T PLAY FAVORITES. SO IN THE KITCHEN THESE ARE MY FAVORITE KITCHEN TOOLS:

SANTOKU KNIFE: (A hollow edged Japanese Chef's knife in both 5-inch and 7-inch) The only knife you need to own. Sharpen it every time you use it and have it professionally sharpened annually. Hold it properly with your pinky, ring & middle fingers holding the handle and thumb & pointer fingers engaging the back of the blade. The 5-inch knife is great if you have small hands.

LONG-HANDLED WHISK: (Also known as a Bar Whisk) A must-have to make the perfect vinaigrette and sauces. The length of the handle allows you to use just your hand to rapidly whisk a creamy blend.

MICROPLANE ZESTER:
Citrus zest is one of my favorite flavorings. No longer do you need to use the "knuckle bleeding" zester. This zester removes only the flavorful surface layer leaving the bitter pith behind. Also use to grate parmesan & chocolate.

LE CREUSET SPATULA:
Can be used in liquids up to 800 degrees. The perfect tool to mix and blend cold or hot dishes and scrape the bowl clean. Don't forget there's always someone who wants to lick the spatula before it goes into the sink.

DEMARLE SILPAT:
Use no other brand. Can be used in the oven up to 480 degrees. A silpat is a patented silicone mat that food does not stick to. Invaluable when baking anything that you place on a cookie sheet. The silpat is an excellent replacement for parchment paper. Simply rinse with water to remove any spills.

OFFSET SPATULA: (Also known as an Angled Knife, in small 4-inch and long 8-inch) A favorite tool to spread butter, jam and icing with ease. The angle makes spreading smooth sailing.

HOMEMADE WOVEN POTHOLDERS:
My daughter Ivy makes them for me. Not only do I love that they are homemade, but they wash and wear like iron. I especially love all of the wonderful color combinations.

ABBREVIATIONS	
Tb-	Tablespoon(s)
tsp-	teaspoon(s)
Cup-	Cup(s)
oz-	ounce(s)
Lb-	pound(s)

TERMINOLOGY

AL DENTE- a term meaning "to-the-tooth" referring to the firmness of pasta or rice.

ALL PURPOSE- referring to flour that can be used in many recipes.

AND/OR- use one or both ingredients to total suggested measure.

BLANCHING- briefly simmering vegetables fork tender

BRAISING LIQUID- a flavorful broth

CHOPPED- the cutting of fruits and vegetables creating uniform, small pieces.

CLOVE- separating a bulb of garlic into its individual parts.

COATING- covering with a thin layer, usually referring to butter or oil.

CONFETTI- cutting a fruit or vegetable into small, uniform pieces that resemble confetti when mixed together.

CRUMBLED- creating small pieces of the ingredient by hand separation from a larger piece.

CUBED- cutting an ingredient into uniform, bite-size squares.

DE-VEINED- the removal of the outside spinal vein, usually referring to shrimp.

DRAINED AND RINSED- place the ingredient in a colander, rinse with cold water and drain excess liquid.

DRIED- dehydrated fruits, herbs and spices that have a longer shelf life than fresh.

FINELY CHOPPED- a very small, uniform dice.

FRESH- an ingredient that is bought and used immediately for the finest recipe results.

FROZEN- the flash freezing of fresh produce, often an acceptable ingredient choice.

GOLDEN- when baking, the desired light brown color is achieved.

GRATED- use a microplane zester resulting in thin, light pieces of the ingredient. Use a box cheese grater for larger, uniform pieces of the ingredient.

HEAD- referring to lettuce in its entirety.

JUICE- extracting the liquid from fruit using a juicer.

JUST UNTIL COMBINED- mixing the ingredients together only until they are incorporated.

LIGHTLY BEATEN- mixing with a whisk prior to incorporating into the recipe.

MELTED- turning a solid, usually butter, into its liquid form.

MINCED- a crushing or chopping that creates very small pieces.

MORE AS NEEDED- adding more of the stated ingredient to enhance the cooking process.

OPTIONAL- an ingredient that you can decide to add or leave out of the recipe.

PASTE- the concentrated form of the ingredient.

PEEL- taking a piece or the entire outside layer off of a vegetable or fruit.

PINCH- grabbing a small amount of the ingredient with your thumb and pointer finger.

PITTED- the removal of the inside pit, usually referring to olives. Easily done by using a cherry pitter.

QUARTERED- cutting the ingredient into four pieces.

ROASTING- cooking a fruit or vegetable at high temperature to enhance rapid caramelization, resulting in a nutty flavor and browning.

SAUTÉ- cooking at high heat to rapidly cook the ingredient.

SECTIONED- peeling and removing the outer pith of citrus fruit, then removing each individual fruit section between the membranes.

SERVING- a suggested number of portions made from a recipe.

SHAVING- using a vegetable peeler to create thin slices of the ingredient.

SIMMER- maintaining steady heat to allow the recipe to cook without boiling or burning.

SKINLESS- the removal of skin, usually referring to meat or seafood.

SMASHED- using a kitchen hammer, strike the ingredient to separate and flatten.

SOAKING- placing an ingredient into a bowl of cold water with the intention of having it soak up the water to soften the ingredient and reduce cooking time.

SOFTENED- when an ingredient is left at room temperature for 30 minutes and becomes soft to touch.

STEMS- woody part of herbs with or without the leaves attached.

STOCK- flavorful broth usually made from chicken, beef, vegetables and seafood.

STORE-BOUGHT- the option to buy a product to substitute for the homemade version.

STRIPS- cutting uniform long, narrow pieces of the ingredient.

TO GARNISH- add an edible herb, flower or fruit slice to the center of the dish. Make sure the garnish is an ingredient in the dish.

TO TASTE- add the amount of the ingredient to your liking.

TOASTED- lightly browned on the stove or in the oven.

UNSWEETENED- containing only the natural sugar of the ingredient, no additional cane sugar added.

VARIATION- a substitution of an ingredient in a recipe leading to a different flavor result.

WHOLE WHEAT- a grain in its most natural state, higher in fiber and flavor.

ZEST- the thin outer layer of citrus fruit removed.

"INHERITING YOUR GRANDMOTHER'S SPICE RACK!"

A STUDENT ONCE TOLD ME SHE INHERITED HER GRANDMOTHER'S SPICE-RACK. MY RESPONSE: "THROW IT OUT!" LOOKING SHOCKED, I WENT ON TO EXPLAIN THAT DRIED HERBS AND SPICES HAVE A VERY SHORT LIFE SPAN TO EXPRESS THEMSELVES IN THEIR FULL GLORY. IF YOU CAN'T SMELL IT YOU CAN'T TASTE IT!

DO...

- Buy small amounts of dried herbs & spices and use them up.
- Cook dried herbs & spices into hot oil and onion. (They relax and release their essence.)
- Use different sizes of ice cream scoops for accurate measure & portion control.
- Bake mini breads & muffins. Smaller portions are in vogue.
- Use a plastic knife to cut hot brownies. My mother's tip that works!
- Cut butter into pieces before melting, it melts quicker.
- Measure a teaspoon of salt in your hand. (You'll never have to measure again except when baking.)
- Use fresh baking powder and baking soda when baking for better results.
- Freeze extra garlic and chopped onion for later use in soups and stews.
- Buy organic fruits, vegetables and meats. (They taste better, are better for you and are worth every penny.)
- Make your grocery list according to the isles in your supermarket. (It's a great time saver.)
- Wash all fruits and vegetables before putting them away in the refrigerator.
- Sharpen your knife every time you use it. (Have them sharpened professionally once a year.)
- Have a weekly menu plan, your family will count on it! (Monday-Vegetarian, Tuesday-Seafood, Wednesday-Rice or Pasta, Thursday- Chicken, Friday- Latin, Saturday- One pot, Sunday- Leftovers)
- Clean out your refrigerator once a week, using up bits and pieces. (It will force you to be creative and you'll make some delicious soups.)
- Add citrus zest to brighten the flavor of dishes and wake up your taste buds.
- Top dishes with fresh herbs or stir them in just before serving. (The exceptions are woody herbs, like thyme and rosemary. Use the entire sprig in soups and stews for flavor.)
- Cook and bake what you enjoy making. (Your family and friends will benefit from you being happy.)
- Use the five-finger rule when entertaining. (Serve only a flavorful main course, interesting whole grain, yummy vegetable, warm bread and a simple salad.)
- Spend time setting a beautiful table. (It makes the food taste better.)
- Add a simple garnish to every dish you serve.
- Check what you have in your pantry and refrigerator before planning a dinner party or evening meal.
- Add flavor when cooking rice, beans or grains. (Instead of water use stock, fruit juice and/or wine.)
- Cook what's in season.

DON'T...

- Over-salt.
- Over-mix or over-bake.
- Over-buy. (Use up what you have and buy fresh.)
- Serve more than two appetizers. (And one or both should be breadsticks, nuts or olives.)
- Open a cookbook when you're entertaining.
  (Reduce your stress by using recipes that you could make in your sleep.)
- Be in the kitchen or worry about the food when you're entertaining.
  (Remember your family and friends want to spend time with you.)
- Ever stop trying new things.
- Underestimate the power of food.

FAVORITE MARKETS, GARDENS & WEBSITES

MY OWN KITCHEN GARDEN
1450 South Harbor Road
Southold, New York
www.farmhousekitchen.us
I only plant lettuce, asparagus, rhubarb, tomatoes, herbs, dahlias and nasturtiums giving me instant freshness at my fingertips. You will find me in the garden with a huge smile on my face. There's no place like home for a Farmer's Daughter.

COMPLEMENT THE CHEF
Route 25
Southold, New York
www.complementthechef.com
Everything you could want in a kitchen store, plus wonderful owners and staff: Meg, Kevin, Joan and Else. If you need it they'll have it or try to get it for you. It's a great place to get your knives sharpened too!

IGA SUPERMARKET
Main Road
Southold, New York
A staff so friendly they will go out of their way to please. I'm especially fond of the meat and produce departments whose workers are willing to fill special requests. The store also carries a decent organic selection. Checking out is a breeze thanks to Alan, Nancy and Maria. Newly renovated, I must admit I miss the old narrow isles and small town style.

SANG LEE FARMS
County Road 48
Cutchogue, New York
www.sangleefarms.com
This family-run farm is the most wonderful, certified-organic vegetable market with the highest quality standards. They also offer a vegetable, fruit and cheese CSA, which is worth every penny you pay for it. I've never been there without seeing Karen and Fred Lee hard at work. Being a Farmer's Daughter, I so appreciate their outstanding contribution to this community.

SOUTHOLD FISH MARKET
Route 25
Southold, New York
Ask for Charlie or Candice who will make sure you have the freshest seafood prepared to your liking. The entire staff always goes the extra mile to please. I've made many early morning requests to make sure the seafood we prepare in classes is extra fresh. I especially like to have a whole fish filleted, reserving the head and bones to make an amazing fish stock, or lobsters with claws removed and tails split ready for the grill. I freeze the lobster bodies then make homemade stock for paella.

THE VILLAGE CHEESE SHOP
Love Lane
Mattituck, New York
www.thevillagecheeseshop.com
You'll find an amazing selection of international and domestic cheeses that you're welcome to taste before making your selection. They also carry those "hard-to-find" ingredients like Israeli couscous and Green Lentils Depuis. Rosemary and Ricardo are always there smiling and ready to please.

UNCLE GIUSEPPE'S
95 Route 111
Smithtown, New York
www.uncleg.com
Calling this an Italian gourmet grocery store doesn't do this amazing store justice. It is a place you have to visit to believe and see the vast array of high quality Italian products. The assortment of pasta, cheeses and olive oils are beyond belief, as is the "jaw-dropping" deli department that goes on for miles.

PENZEYS SPICES
Grand Central Station, New York City
www.penzeys.com
Penzeys is a great resource for fresh dried herbs, spices and innovative spice blends. It's worth the trip to Grand Central to experience the exquisite assortment and be treated to a wealth of information while smelling to your hearts content.

FAVORITE MARKETS, GARDENS & WEBSITES

KALUSTYANS
123 Lexington Avenue, New York City
www.kalustyans.com
The international cuisine "candy store" where you can spend the entire day lost in different parts of the world. Park close by and bring your reusable bags to carry the heavy load of goodies you'll be sure to purchase. The variety of rice and beans alone will make you jump for joy. I buy all of my Indian cuisine products there and always have lunch upstairs at their multi-cultural café.

ASIA MARKET CORPORATION
71 1/2 Mulberry Street, New York City
Located in lower Chinatown, this is the ultimate Asian market and well worth the trip. Filled with every variety of noodle, rice and seasoning you will need to transform your kitchen into a Thai, Indonesian, Vietnamese, Malaysian, Japanese or Chinese restaurant. Plan to spend the day and try to park close because you won't be able to resist all that the Asia Market has to offer.

THE ESSEX MARKET
120 Essex Street, New York City
www.essexsteetmarket.com
www.saxelbycheese.com
This long time Latin market has been rediscovered in the last few years and is now exploding with new innovative purveyors. My personal favorite is Saxelby Cheesemongers, which has cornered a niche in outstanding American Farmstead cheeses. Petite in size, you'll find it just as you enter the market. Latin produce and gourmet shops abounding, this market will steal your day and fill your bags with freshness. This cutting edge market is a gem.

WHOLE FOODS MARKET
429 North Broadway
Jericho, New York
(Across from the Smith Haven Mall and numerous New York City locations)
www.wholefoodsmarket.com
Located everywhere except the North Fork of Long Island this is the ultimate, organic fresh food market. The depth and plentiful variety of whole and natural foods is mind-boggling. But once you've shopped at a Whole Foods Market, you'll make the long trip back because it's worth it!

CROTEAUX VINEYARDS
1450 South Harbor Road
Southold, New York
www.croteaux.com
Our charming French tasting barn and garden where we serve only dry, French-style Rosés, play only French music and guarantee you'll feel like you're in Provence. We are proud to be the only vineyard in the United States dedicated to making only quality, boutique rosé wines.

"THANK YOU"

LETTIE TEAGUE- My newest neighbor and friend, whose willingness to extend her hand and heart has touched me. RACHEL CRONEMEYER- The perfect kitchen partner, whose love of food and typing made this cookbook possible. FRANCESCA BOCHNER- A perfectionist extraordinaire who edited every inch of this cookbook. KATE RATHBUN- Who left too soon to "follow her heart," but was a great contributor to recipe organization. ELSE MARIE QUIST- My graceful friend and long time kitchen companion, for always being there. PAT SANDERS- My friend with "asbestos hands" and much wisdom. CAROL BEAUGARD- My dear friend and gentle listener who loves to entertain as much as I do. MEG HOCHSTRASSER, KEVIN SHANNON and JOAN SHANNON (owners of Compliment the Chef) - for creating an incredible kitchen store and for always offering a discount. And to all my students... THANK YOU!

THIS COOKBOOK INCLUDES MANY RECIPES THAT HAVE BEEN PASSED ALONG. THESE RECIPES HAVE STOOD THE TEST OF TIME AND PLEASED MANY A CROWD. THERE ARE A FEW FRIENDS AND FAMILY THAT I'D LIKE TO ESPECIALLY THANK:

JANE FRANKE- Someone who loved to cook, bake & entertain more than anyone I know. CHRIS HILLIKER- The warmest home in Vermont and someone who truly loves to cook for her family. AUNT HELEN- Who was ahead of her time as a master chef and who made so many firemen happy. 'GRAMMY' PEARL REIDY- The most gracious and loving person who cherished her family and home. I treasure your hand written recipe book. BABCHI SKWARA & BABCHI MARKISZ- For letting me be your kitchen "sponge", and for teaching me that food and especially the preparation of it, is love. My daughter IVY JANE- Who has the taste of an angel and an exquisite palette too. Thank you for being you and keeping me on my toes in and out of the kitchen. My son MARKIS REIDY- My very best taste tester. Your enthusiasm for what I create touches me, and yes I know that chocolate chips belong in everything. And last, but oh so not least, my mother JOYCE SKWARA- Who has scrubbed every pot & dish that I own. Thank you for encouraging me by making me feel that I could do anything and for always just eating the crust. You are the perfect mother.

"PURÉED CARDBOARD"

I WOULD BE REMISS IN NOT THANKING MY INCREDIBLE HUSBAND MICHAEL. WITHOUT YOU THIS FARMHOUSE DREAM WOULD NOT HAVE BEEN. WE HAVE LIVED AND LOVED THE PROCESS OF BUILDING OUR HOME & FAMILY FOR THE LAST 20 YEARS. CREATING A VERY FULL LIFE (YES SOMETIMES TOO FULL). SEEING THE WORLD THROUGH THE "SAME COLORED GLASSES" IS WHY I HAVE BEEN ABLE TO BECOME WHO I AM. THANK YOU FOR DESIGNING AND PHOTOGRAPHING MY FIRST COOKBOOK. I LEARNED AND LOVED EVERY MINUTE OF WORKING WITH YOU. THIS COOKBOOK AND THE LENGTHY PROCESS OF CREATING IT SPEAKS TO OUR HARMONY. I CAN'T SAY THAT I COOK FOR YOU, BECAUSE QUITE HONESTLY, YOU REALLY ARE NOT THAT INTERESTED IN FOOD. ON THE CONTRARY, I OFTEN JOKE THAT YOU WOULD BE PERFECTLY HAPPY WITH "PUREED CARDBOARD." INSTEAD YOU APPRECIATE THE "ART" IN COOKING AND THE "SPEED" AT WHICH IT CAN BE DONE. YOU HAVE OFTEN SAID THAT I MAKE A WONDERFUL TWENTY-MINUTE MEAL FROM NOTHING. YOU INSPIRE ME TO BE THE VERY BEST WIFE, MOTHER, DAUGHTER, SISTER, FRIEND AND EVEN COOK.

INDEX

A

Apple Cake, Jane's, 123
Apple Crisp, Farmhouse, 127
Asian Salmon,
    Glazed with Mint and Lime Tartar Sauce, 103
Asparagus Salad, Roasted, 51
Aunt Helen's Macaroni and Cheese, 87

APPLES
Caramel Apples, 135
Farmhouse Apple Crisp, 127
Jane's Apple Cake, 123

B

Baked Beans, Farmhouse, 69
Banana Chocolate Chip Bread, 149
Barbecued Chorizo, 23
Basmati Rice, Coconut, 55
Beef Stew with Gremolata, Farmhouse, 73
Black Bean Vegetable Chili with Cheddar Biscuits, 85
Blackberry Jam Cupcakes, 115
Blueberry Crumb Tart and Flaky Pie Crust, 121
Brownies, Espresso Kahlua, 117
Buttermilk Biscuits, Farmhouse, 139
Butters, Flavored, 141, 147

BEANS
Black Bean Vegetable Chili with Cheddar Biscuits, 85
Cooking Dried Beans, 67
Farmhouse Baked Beans, 69
White Bean & Tuna Salad, 67

BREAD
Banana Chocolate Chip Bread, 149
Cheese Babka, 145
Corny Corn Bread, 147
Irish Soda Bread, 143

C

Caramel Apples, 135
Carrot Ginger Soup, 43
Cassoulet, Farmhouse, 81
Cheddar Biscuits, 85
Cheddar Cheese Crackers, 25
Cheese Babka, 145
Cheese Spread, Farmhouse, 13
Chicken Casserole with Phyllo Roses, 89
Chicken Pot Pie, 75
Chocolate Truffles, 125
Citrus Couscous 57
Coconut Basmati Rice, 55
Coq au Vin Blanc, 83

Corny Corn Bread, 147
Croteaux Rosé Sangria, 33
Cucumber and Fresh Herb Salsa, 103
Cupcakes, Blackberry Jam, 115

CHEESE
Aunt Helen's Macaroni and Cheese, 87
Cheddar Biscuits, 85
Cheddar Cheese Crackers, 25
Cheese Babka, 145
Creamy Blue Cheese Dressing, 49
Farmhouse Cheese Spread, 13
Feta with Roasted Grapes, 17

CHICKEN
Chicken Casserole with Phyllo Roses, 89
Chicken Pot Pie, 75
Coq au Vin Blanc, 83
Farmhouse Cassoulet, 81
Rosemary Chicken, 99
Stuffed Chicken Breast with Red Grape Puree, 93

CHOCOLATE
Banana Chocolate Chip Bread, 149
Chocolate Truffles, 125
Espresso Kahlua Brownies, 117

COCONUT
Coconut Basmati Rice, 55
Mussels in Coconut Curry Sauce, 105

E

Eggplant Caponata, 21
English Currant Scones with Flavored Butters, 141
Espresso Kahlua Brownies, 117

F

Feta with Roasted Grapes, 17
Flaky Pie Crust, 121
Flavored Butters, 141, 147
French Toast, Stuffed Croissant, 137

FARMHOUSE
Farmhouse Apple Crisp, 127
Farmhouse Baked Beans, 69
Farmhouse Beef Stew with Gremolata, 73
Farmhouse Buttermilk Biscuits with Lemon Curd, 139
Farmhouse Cassoulet, 81
Farmhouse Cheese Spread, 13
Farmhouse Green Salad, 45
Farmhouse Vinaigrettes, 45

INDEX

FAVORITES
Abbreviations, 150
Dos & Don'ts, 153
In My Pantry, 150
Kitchen Tools, 151
Recipe Terms, 152
Stores, Markets, Gardens & Websites, 154-155

FRUIT
Banana Chocolate Chip Bread, 149
Blackberry Jam Cupcakes, 115
Blueberry Crumb Tart, 121
Caramel Apples, 135
Citrus Couscous, 57
Farmhouse Apple Crisp, 127
Feta with Roasted Grapes, 17
Grapefruit, Fennel & Arugula Salad, 47
Green Grape Salsa, 15
Jane's Apple Cake, 123
Lemon Curd, 139
Lemon Squares, 119
Maple Blueberry Compote, 137
Orange Salsa, 109
Poached White Fish with Fennel and Apples, 107
Red Grape Puree, 93
Roasted Nuts & Fruit, 31
Very Berry Cobbler, 129

G
Glazed Asian Salmon with Mint and
  Lime Tartar Sauce, 103
Grapefruit, Fennel & Arugula Salad, 47
Greek Tabbouleh, 63
Green Grape Salsa, 15
Green Salad and Vinaigrettes, Farmhouse, 45
Gremolata, 73
Grilled Garlic Shrimp and Orange Salsa, 109

H
Honey Sage Pork Chops, 97

HERBS
Gremolata with Parsley, Mint or Cilantro, 73
Honey Sage Pork Chops, 97
Mint and Lime Tartar Sauce, 103
Sea Scallops on Rosemary Skewers, 111
Zucchini Basil Soup, 41

I
Iceberg Wedge & Creamy Blue Cheese Dressing, 49
Irish Soda Bread, 143

J
Jalapeno Butter, 147
Jane's Apple Cake, 123

L
Lamb Shank, Moroccan, 79
Lemon Curd, 139
Lemon Squares, 119

M
Macaroni & Cheese, Aunt Helen's, 87
Maple Blueberry Compote, 137
Mint and Lime Tartar Sauce, 103
Moroccan Lamb Shank, 79
Mussels in Coconut Curry Sauce, 105

MEATS
Barbecued Chorizo 23
Farmhouse Beef Stew with Gremolata, 73
Farmhouse Cassoulet, 81
Honey Sage Pork Chops, 97
Moroccan Lamb Shank, 79
Southern Barbecue Ribs, 101
Thai Turkey Burger with Wasabi Mayonnaise, 95

N
North Fork Potato & Leek Soup, 37
Nuts & Fruit, Roasted, 31

O
Oatmeal Pancakes with Caramel Apples, 135
Olives with a Twist, 29
Orange Salsa, 109
Outrageous Cookies, 131

P
Paella, Seafood, 77
Pancakes, Oatmeal, 135
Phyllo Roses, Chicken Casserole, 89
Pilaf, Saffron Quinoa, 61
Poached White Fish with Fennel and Apples, 107
Potato & Leek Soup, North Fork, 37
Pork Chops, Honey Sage, 97
Potato Pancakes, 97

Q
Quinoa, Saffron Pilaf, 61

INDEX

R
Red Grape Puree, 93
Red Onion Galette, 27
Roasted Asparagus Salad, 51
Roasted Nuts & Fruit, 31
Rosé Sangria, Croteaux , 33
Rosemary Chicken, 99

ROASTED
Roasted Asparagus Salad, 51
Roasted Grapes with Feta, 17
Roasted Nuts & Fruit, 31

RICE
Coconut Basmati Rice, 55
Wild Rice Salad, 59

S
Saffron Quinoa Pilaf, 61
Salmon, Glazed Asian, 103
Scones, English Currant, 141
Seafood Corn Chowder, 39
Seafood Paella, 77
Sea Scallops on Rosemary Skewers, 111
Southern Barbecue Ribs, 101
Spinach Gratin, 99
Stuffed Chicken Breast with Red Grape Puree, 93
Stuffed Croissant French Toast with Maple Blueberry
Compote, 137
Swiss Chard, 93

SEAFOOD
Glazed Asian Salmon with Mint
  and Lime Tartar Sauce, 103
Grilled Garlic Shrimp and Orange Salsa, 109
Mussels in Coconut Curry Sauce, 105
Poached White Fish with Fennel and Apples, 107
Sea Scallops on Rosemary Skewers, 111
Seafood Paella, 77
White Bean & Tuna Salad, 67

SOUP
Carrot Ginger Soup, 43
North Fork Potato & Leek Soup, 37
Seafood Corn Chowder, 39
Zucchini Basil Soup, 41

SALAD
Farmhouse Green Salad and Vinaigrettes, 45
Grapefruit, Fennel & Arugula Salad, 47
Greek Tabbouleh, 63
Iceberg Wedge & Creamy Blue Cheese Dressing, 49

Roasted Asparagus Salad, 51
Wheat Berry Confetti Salad, 65
White Bean & Tuna Salad, 67

T
Thai Turkey Burger with Wasabi Mayonnaise, 95
Tabbouleh, Greek, 63
Tuna Salad & White Beans, 67

V
Very Berry Cobbler, 129
Vinaigrette, 45
Vinaigrette, Asian, 95
Vinaigrette, Farmhouse, 45

VEGETABLES
Asparagus Salad, Roasted, 51
Carrot Ginger Soup, 43
Cucumber and Fresh Herb Salsa, 103
Eggplant Caponata, 21
Fennel and Apples with Poached White Fish, 107
Fennel & Arugula Salad with Grapefruit, 47
Green Salad, Farmhouse, 45
Iceberg Wedge & Creamy Blue Cheese Dressing, 49
Potato & Leek Soup, North Fork, 37
Potato Pancakes, 97
Red Onion Galette, 27
Spinach Gratin, 99
Swiss Chard, 93
Vegetable Chili with Black Beans, 85
Zucchini Basil Soup, 41
Zucchini Quiche, 19

W
Wasabi Mayonnaise, 95
Wheat Berry Confetti Salad, 65
White Bean & Tuna Salad, 67
Wild Rice Salad, 59

Z
Zucchini Basil Soup, 41
Zucchini Quiche, 19